EFFECTIVE CHURCH LEADERSHIP

A Practical Sourcebook

HARRIS W. LEE

AUGSBURG/MINNEAPOLIS

EFFECTIVE CHURCH LEADERSHIP
A Practical Sourcebook

Library of Congress Cataloging-in-Publication Data

Lee, Harris W.
    Effective church leadership : a practical sourcebook / Harris W.
Lee.
        p.   cm.
    Bibliography: p.
    ISBN 0-8066-2423-X
    1. Christian leadership.   I. Title.
BV652.1.L44   1989
253—dc19   89-6486
                                                        CIP

Manufactured in the U.S.A.   AF 9-2423

93   92   91   90   89   1   2   3   4   5   6   7   8   9   10

To the members of
Lutheran Church of the Good Shepherd
in Minneapolis,
who gave me a summer sabbatical to read and write.

To Paul Hanson,
Ryan LaHurd, Roland Seboldt,
Merv Thompson, and Doris Yock,
who read, critiqued, and suggested.

To Maryon,
whose encouragement and patience
helped sustain my perseverance.

CONTENTS

CONTENTS

ACKNOWLEDGMENTS

Excerpts from *Leadership* by James MacGregor Burns are copyright © 1978 by James MacGregor Burns and reprinted by permission of Harper & Row, Publishers, Inc.

Excerpts from *Servant Leadership* by Robert Greenleaf (New York: Paulist Press) are copyright © 1977 and used by permission of the publisher.

Material from "What About Teaching Leadership?" by Edward Wynne, *AGB Reports* (March–April 1984), pp. 38–39 is used by permission of the publisher.

Excerpts from *Real Power* by Janet Hagberg are copyright © 1984 by the author and reprinted by permission of Harper & Row, Publishers, Inc.

The Managerial Grid figure from *The Managerial Grid III: The Key to Leadership Excellence* by Robert R. Blake and Jane Srygley Mouton (Houston: Gulf Publishing Company) is copyright © 1985, page 12, and reproduced by permission.

Material from *The Decision Makers* by Lyle E. Schaller (Nashville: Abingdon Press) is copyright © 1974 and used by permission of the publisher.

The exhibit from "How to Choose a Leadership Pattern" by Robert Tannebaum and Warren H. Schmidt is reprinted by permission of *Harvard Business Review* (May/June 1973) and copyright © 1973 by the President and Fellows of Harvard College; all rights reserved.

Material from *The Situational Leader* by Paul Hersey (New York: Warner Books, 1984) is copyrighted material from Leadership Studies, Inc.; all rights reserved; used by permission.

"Four Leadership Styles" (excerpted and abridged) and chart from pp. 57 and 68 of *Leadership and the One Minute Manager* by Kenneth Blanchard, Ph.D., Patricia Zigarmi, Ed.D., and Drea Zigarmi, Ed. D., is copyright © 1985 by Blanchard Management Corporation and used by permission of William Morrow and Company, Inc.

Material from *Getting Things Done* by Lyle E. Schaller (Nashville: Abingdon Press) is copyright © 1986 and used by permission of the publisher.

ACKNOWLEDGMENTS

"The Jo-Hari Window" is from *Group Processes* by Joseph Luft and used by permission of Mayfield Publishing Company. Copyright © 1984, 1970, 1963 by Joseph Luft.

"The Awareness Wheel" is from *Couple Communication I: Talking Together* by Sherod Miller, Elam W. Nunnally, and Daniel B. Wackman, and is used by permission of Interpersonal Communications Programs, Littleton, Colorado. For more information, see *Connecting with Self and Others* by Miller et al. Call 1-800-328-5099.

"The Myers-Briggs Type Indicator" is adapted from *Please Understand Me* by David Keirsey and Marilyn Bates (Del Mar, CA: Gnosology Books, 1984) and is used by permission of Prometheus Nemesis Book Co.

Material from "The Church as Platypus" by Philip Yancey is used by permission of the author.

Material from *Wheel Within the Wheel* by Richard G. Hutcheson Jr. (Atlanta: John Knox Press) is copyright © 1979 and used by permission of the author.

Material from *Ministry and Management* by Peter Rudge is copyright © 1968 and used by permission of Tavistock Publications.

Material from *Power and Innocence: A Search for the Sources of Violence* by Rollo May is used by permission of W. W. Norton & Co., Inc. and copyright © 1972 by Rollo May.

Material from *Synergic Power* by James H. Craig and Marguerite Craig (Berkeley: Proactive Press) is copyright © 1979 and used by permission of the authors.

Material from *Leadership: Definitions, Dimensions, Directions* by Robert Terry (Minneapolis: University Media Resources) is copyright © 1979 and used by permission of the author.

Excerpt from *Money, Sex & Power* by Richard J. Foster is copyright © 1985 by Richard J. Foster and reprinted by permission of Harper & Row, Publishers, Inc.

Material from "Four Traits of Leadership" by Warren Bennis in *The Leader-Manager* (John N. Williamson, ed.) is copyright © 1984 by John Wiley & Sons and reprinted by permission of John Wiley & Sons, Inc.

Material from *Megatrends* by John Naisbitt is reprinted with permission of Warner Books, Inc., New York and copyright © 1984 by John Naisbitt.

Material from *Feminine Leadership: Or How to Succeed in Business without Being One of the Boys* by Marilyn Loden (New York: Times Books) is copyright © 1985 and used by permission of the publisher.

ACKNOWLEDGMENTS

Material from *Re-inventing the Corporation* by John Naisbitt and Patricia Aburdene is reprinted with permission of Warner Books/New York and is copyright © 1985 by Megatrends, Ltd.

"The Androgynous Leader Quiz" from *Applied Management Newsletter* 8 (Jan. 1985) is used by permission of the National Association of Management.

Material from "The Ministry Today: A Survey of Perspectives" by Richard D. Vangerud in *Word & World* 1 (Fall 1981): 391–97 is used by permission of the publisher.

Material from "Ten Models of Ordained Ministry" by Margaret Fletcher Clark and Loren Mead is reprinted by permission from *Action Information*, published by The Alban Institute, Inc., 4125 Nebraska Avenue, NW, Washington, DC 20016; copyright 1985, 1983; all rights reserved.

Material from *The Center Letter* 2/13 & 14 (Nov. & Dec. 1972) is used by permission of The Center for Parish Development. The Center for Parish Development is a church research agency focusing on the processes of planned transformation. *The Center Letter* is a monthly research publication available on a subscription basis.

Material from *Applied Management Newsletter* 7 (Aug. 1984) is used by permission of the National Association for Management.

Material from *Strategy for Leadership* by Edward R. Dayton and Ted W. Engstrom is copyright © 1979 by Fleming H. Revell Company. Used by permission of the Fleming H. Revell Company.

Material from *Effective Church Planning* by Lyle E. Schaller (Nashville: Abingdon Press) is copyright © 1979 and used by permission of the publisher.

Excerpts from p. 166 of *Building Effective Ministry* by Carl S. Dudley are copyright © 1983 by Carl S. Dudley and reprinted by permission of Harper & Row, Publishers, Inc.

The poem on p. 144 is copyright © 1972 by Lake Publishing Company.

Data (for diagram) based on Hierarchy of Needs from "A Theory of Motivation" in *Motivation and Personality*, third edition, by Abraham H. Maslow and revised by Robert Frager et al. is copyright 1954, 1987 by Harper & Row, Publishers, and copyright © by Abraham H. Maslow; reprinted·by permission of Harper & Row, Publishers, Inc.

"Motivation-Hygiene Theory" in *Work and the Nature of Man* by Frederick Herzberg is copyright © 1966 and used by permission of the author.

Material from *Work and Motivation* by Victor Vroom is copyright © 1964 by John Wiley & Sons and reprinted by permission of John Wiley & Sons, Inc.

ACKNOWLEDGMENTS

Material reprinted from *Training Volunteer Leaders* is reprinted with the permission of the YMCA of the USA, 101 North Wacker Drive, Chicago, IL 60606.

The quote by David Bandey on pp. 158-59 is used by permission of *Journal of Theology for Southern Africa*.

"Checklist for Diagnosing Conflict" from *Applied Management Newsletter* 10 (Dec. 1986):1 is used by permission of the National Association for Management.

Material from "When Conflict Erupts in Your Church" by Speed Leas is reprinted by permission from *Action Information*, published by The Alban Institute, Inc., 4125 Nebraska Ave., NW, Washington, DC 20016; copyright 1985, 1983; all rights reserved.

Material from "Conflict in the Parish: How Bad Is It?" by Speed Leas in *Word & World* 4 (Spring 1984): 182-91 is used by permission of the publisher.

Material from *Getting to Yes* by Roger Fisher and William Ury is copyright © 1981 by Roger Fisher and William Ury and reprinted by permission of Houghton Mifflin Company.

Material from *The Professional Manager* by Douglas MacGregor is used by permission of McGraw-Hill Publishing Company, copyright © 1967.

Material from "The Pastoral Calling from the Perspective of a Bishop" by Herbert W. Chilstrom in *Word & World* 1 (Fall 1985):335 is used by permission of the publisher.

"I Need Thy Sense of Order" from *Deep is the Hunger* by Howard Thurman is copyright © 1956 and used by permission of Friends United Press.

Material from *Let God Love You* by Lloyd John Ogilvie is copyright © 1984 and used by permission of the publisher, Word Books, Dallas, Texas.

INTRODUCTION

Why do some churches thrive while others languish? Why are some vital and purposeful while others flounder? I am sure the reasons are many, among them the makeup of the community; the quality of the congregational life, especially its worship and preaching; the program and fellowship opportunities; and the prayers and participation of the people.

After more than 25 years as a parish pastor in three different congregations, I conclude that there is another factor that is not often discussed. I refer to the leadership factor: the quality, quantity, and timeliness of the leadership exercised by pastors and elected leaders of congregations.

This book is intended to strengthen the leadership of the church (and, subsequently, the church's life and mission) by providing a better understanding of leadership and how it can be practiced effectively by pastors and lay leaders.

It describes qualities of church leaders, discusses the leadership roles of pastors and lay people, highlights some of the latest insights on motivation and conflict management, and considers the leader's personal life and spiritual development. The book is an overview of leadership ideas, a distillation of the insights of many.

It is a sampler of leadership theory and practice. It intends to open doors to further study, to guide continuing reflection and practice.

Leadership has been the subject of a great deal of study and writing during the past 50 years. James MacGregor Burns says it is "one of the most observed and least understood phenomena on earth."[1] Warren Bennis and Burt Nanus, whose book *Leaders* is based on a study of 90 top executives in the public and private sectors, state that despite decades of academic analysis there are at least 350 definitions of leadership.[2] *Stogdill's Handbook of Leadership*, a survey of theory and research on the subject revised and expanded by Bernard M. Bass, is 618 pages long, and has a bibliography of 189 pages, listing nearly 4000 published books and articles on the subject.

When he had completed his examination of several thousand books and articles, Ralph Stogdill said:

> Four decades of research on research have produced a bewildering mass of findings. Numerous surveys of special problems have been published, but they seldom include all the studies available on a topic. It is difficult to know what, if anything, has been convincingly demonstrated by replicated research. The endless accumulation of empirical data has not produced an integrated understanding of leadership.[3]

Theologian Paul Tillich wrote of the ambiguity of leadership which he said runs through all human relations, from the parent–child to the ruler–subject relationship. The ambiguity, he noted, is over the tension between creativity and destruction that characterizes all life processes.[4] But not only does this add to the complexity of the subject, it contributes to its appeal, serving as a lure to further study and discussion.

The subject is of interest because of its importance. Some speak of the crisis of leadership, pointing to perceived inadequacies of government, of business, of social and volunteer organizations, including the church. "The crisis of leadership today is the mediocrity or irresponsibility of so many of the men and women in power," writes James Burns. He adds that the fundamental crisis underlying the mediocrity is intellectual. We know too little about leadership, says Burns.

> We fail to grasp the essence of leadership that is relevant to the modern age and hence we cannot agree on even the standards by which to measure, recruit, and reject it. Is leadership simply innovation—cultural or political? Is it essentially inspiration? Mobilization of followers? Goal setting? Goal fulfillment? Is a leader the definer of values? Satisfier of needs? If leaders require followers, who leads whom from where to where, and why? How do leaders lead followers without being wholly led by followers? Leadership is one of the most observed and least understood phenomena on earth.[5]

The crisis in leadership is as evident in the church as it is anywhere. While the church can often muddle through despite the ineptitude of its leaders, the right kind and quality of leadership has a significant role in bridging the gap between what is and what can be—resulting in a church that is more faithful to its Lord than it would otherwise be.

Leadership has been practiced from earliest days, and not least of all among the people of God. Such biblical persons as Moses, Joshua, David, Deborah, Peter, and Paul were, among other things, leaders. They did not use the same style of leadership, nor lead under identical circumstances, nor achieve the same results, but it is evident that they exercised leadership responsibilities.

A quick review of the history of the early church reveals the same truth: some were leaders. Clement of Rome, Irenaeus of Lyons, Cyprian of Carthage, Ignatius of Antioch, Augustine of Hippo—all were leaders in the early centuries of the church. From the Middle Ages, such names as Luther, Calvin, and Melanchthon come quickly to mind; and in the present era are Dietrich Bonhoeffer, Martin Luther King Jr., and Dorothy Day. Gifted in different ways, they nevertheless are remembered largely for the influence of their leadership. Edward Schillebeeckx sums it up with a quotation attributed to the church father Jerome: "There can be no church community without a leader or team of leaders."[6]

Despite this, however, much of the recent literature on the general subject has been oriented not toward leadership but toward management. Perhaps this is because management seems to be more in keeping with the servant posture and self-image of church people. To be a manager is to be a servant or steward—appropriate self-images for one who would follow Christ. To be a leader is to be subject to the pitfalls of pride and arrogance.

Yet in recent years a number of books have been published with the word "leadership" in the title, and many authors speak forthrightly about the need for leadership in today's institutions. This emphasis is also evident in the church. Kennon Callahan states flatly, "The time for leaders has come, the time for enablers is past."[7] The distinction Warren Bennis makes between management and leadership is good: "Management is doing things in the right way; leadership is doing the right thing." In the church, too, doing things in the right way is important; but of even greater importance is doing the right thing—the essential function of leadership.

My task and venture has been to comb through some of the best writings on the subject, much of it secular—that is, without reference to God—and gather insights and principles that seem useful for the church. The "best writings" I refer to were determined by polling 80 leaders from education, business, church, government, and health care institutions. Many of the same titles appeared again and again on the lists of the 50 or so who responded to my invitation to submit suggestions.

While drawing from secular writings may surprise some, it is well to remember that the church has often used insights from the secular world to further its cause—philosophy to interpret its message, speech to proclaim it, psychology to enhance its pastoral care, and organizational development to strengthen its administration. The leadership skills and knowledge required in other disciplines are essentially the same as those required in the church. Learnings may be borrowed, techniques may be transferred. Moreover, the secular world is also God's realm and where God rules. Our Lord's parable of the dishonest steward, commended for his prudence, would seem to say, "Christian, learn from the world!" (Luke 16:1–8).

In Part One, I consider the subject of leadership from a biblical perspective, viewing it as a gift and calling from God, and as a ministry to and by God's people. I then clarify the primary functions of leadership, state a general definition, and consider several different leadership theories.

Part Two focuses on the importance of knowing yourself, your group, and the appropriate use of power and authority.

In Part Three, I turn to the people who lead, highlighting some of the marks and qualities that seem most appropriate for use in the church, then clarifying the leadership role and responsibilities of pastors and elected lay leaders. Here I also discuss and advocate the development of leadership teams.

In Part Four, I take up the everyday tasks of leadership: planning, motivating, and managing conflict; coordinating, organizing, and staffing; and provide insights for the effective accomplishment of these tasks.

Part Five focuses on the relationship of spirituality and leadership, using insights from secular authors on the subject while emphasizing the resources of the Christian faith.

The Afterword says there is much more to consider, more to learn on the subject, more to assimilate and apply in the life of the church. The subject of leadership is finally open-ended. Yet it is the means through which God's purposes are so often fulfilled.

PART ONE

LEADERSHIP
AND
LEADERS

Perhaps the most appealing reason for believing in the concept of leadership is that we all deeply want to believe that somewhere, some place, right now, leadership is happening. Somewhere great dreams are being energized, somewhere great thoughts are being put into action. . . . How else will wars be ended, will people be fed and housed, will the edge of scientific knowledge be extended outward, will the ultimate frontier of space be explored?

David P. Campbell

A spiritual gift is the call of God, addressed to an individual, to a particular ministry in the community, which brings with it the ability to fulfill that ministry.

Hans Küng

1

A GIFT,
A CALLING,
A MINISTRY

Leadership in the church may use insights from the secular world, but it is rooted in the faith "once delivered to the saints." Church leaders may quote James Burns, Warren Bennis, Peter Drucker, and Tom Peters, but they are inspired by the Lord of the church, by the prophets and apostles, and by the fact that leadership is a gift, a calling, and a ministry.

A GIFT

The New Testament is clear in stating that the church is a gifted community. It owes its very existence to a gift—the gospel of Christ. Its faith, its hope, its love, and the promises by which it lives are also seen as gifts. The men and women who made up the early church were manifestations of God's gifts.

Note what the following New Testament passages say about such gifts:

Now there are varieties of gifts, but the same Spirit; and there are varieties of working, but it is the same God who inspires them all in every one. To each is given the manifestation of the Spirit for the common good. To one is given through the Spirit the utterance of wisdom, and to another the utterance of knowledge according to the same Spirit, to another faith by the same Spirit, to another gifts of healing by the one Spirit, to another the working of mira- cles, to another prophecy, to another the ability to distinguish between spirits, to another the interpretation of tongues. All these are inspired by one and the same Spirit, who apportions to each one individually as he wills.

(1 Cor. 12:4-11)

For as in one body we have many members, and all the members do not have the same function, so we, though many, are one body in Christ, and individually members one of another. Having gifts that differ according to the grace given to us, let us use them: if prophecy, in proportion to our faith; if service, in our serving; he who teaches, in his teaching; he who exhorts, in his exhortation; he who con- tributes, in liberality; he who gives aid, with zeal; he who does acts of mercy, with cheerfulness.

(Rom. 12:4-8)

And his gifts were that some should be apostles, some prophets, some evangelists, some pastors and teachers, to equip the saints for the work of ministry, for building up the body of Christ, until we all attain to the unity of the faith and the knowledge of the Son of God, to mature manhood, to the measure of the stature of the fulness of Christ.

(Eph. 4:11-13)

While God's gifts to the church are many and varied, they are given for the common good, for the sake of the life, well-being, and mission of the church. Some of the gifts are spiritual—faith, for example, or knowledge of the Son of God. Others are what we would call talents or abilities—preaching and teaching, for example. In addition to the more obvious tasks of ministry are gifts that fall under the category of administration. These are suggested later in the Corinthian passage: "God has appointed in the church first apostles, second prophets, third teachers, then

workers of miracles, then healers, helpers, administrators . . . "
(1 Cor. 12:28).

Another way of saying it would be to say that God hereby appointed leaders for the church, leaders functioning in different capacities and in order to evoke and direct the gifts of others for the well-being of the church and its mission. The Corinthians were not lacking in any spiritual gift, but they did lack the order and unity that would coordinate and direct the use of the many gifts God had given. In other words, they lacked leadership.

Other New Testament writings refer to the work of stewards, elders, deacons, and bishops—all of them leaders in the early church, and all of them seen as gifts to the church for the sake of its well-being and mission. Concludes Edward Schillebeeckx: "It can no longer be denied that towards the end of the first century there was a church order according to which a group of presbyters was responsible for the leadership and pastoral care of the local communities."[1]

What was true in the past is true today. In the Evangelical Lutheran Church in America, for example, the official documents acknowledge that some in the church have leadership responsibilities, and then describe in general terms how they are to be exercised: "Leaders in this church should demonstrate that they are servants by their words, life-style, and manner of leadership."[2] Letters of call extended by congregations to pastors also commonly refer to the leadership responsibility of the pastor. The call is to exercise leadership in the congregation as well as to preach, teach, administer the sacraments, and provide pastoral care.

This is not to diminish the servant role of Christ's followers, leaders included. The quotation in the previous paragraph from the constitution of the Evangelical Lutheran Church in America states clearly that the leadership role is to be exercised in a servant posture. More will be said about this in the next chapter and later when the "servant-leader" concept popularized by Robert Greenleaf is discussed. Here it is enough to emphasize that leadership is one of God's gifts to the church. Whether chosen by the personal invitation of Jesus, as in the case of the first disciples, the casting of lots for Mathias to replace Judas, as in the early church, or through the interviews and congregational votes of to-day's church, leadership is one of God's gifts to the church.

A CALLING

In his bimonthly newsletter, *Context*, Martin Marty quotes businessman-friend, James A. Autry, on the subject of manage-ment. Management, says Autry, is a sacred trust, an art, a calling. The same can be said for leadership. So, as you read his state-ments below, substitute the word "leadership" for "management":

> Work can provide the opportunity for spiritual and personal, as well as financial, growth. If it doesn't then we're wasting too much of our lives on it. The workplace is rapidly becoming a new neigh-borhood, and American businesspeople are helping to make it happen. Good management is largely a matter of love. Or if you're uncomfortable with that word, call it caring, because proper man-agement involves caring for people, not manipulating them.
>
> Management is a sacred trust in which the well-being of people is put in your care during most of their waking hours. It is a trust placed upon you first by those who put you in the job, but more important than that, it is a trust placed upon you after you get the job by those whom you are to manage.

Autry describes two kinds of managers: those who practice management as a trainable skill with all sorts of technical and administrative aspects that, when pursued properly, serve to di-rect people in performing in the company's best interest; and those who approach management as a calling.[3]

The two kinds of management or leadership are not, however, mutually exclusive. Later chapters will show that learned skills enhance the ability to fulfill the leadership calling, evoke and perfect the gift that is often more of a latent capacity than a usable ability. Here we focus on the idea that leadership is a calling.

The concept of the call is important in our tradition. In the Old Testament God called people into a covenant relationship, the basis of which is stated as follows: "It was not because you were more in number than any other people that the Lord set his love upon you and chose you, for you were the fewest of all peoples; but it is because the Lord loves you . . . " (Deut. 7:7-8a). Their commission, in turn, was to be a blessing to others: "And by your descendants shall all the nations of the earth bless themselves, because you have obeyed my voice" (Gen. 22:18). Such is vocation in the Old Testament: the calling of Israel to be God's people for the fulfillment of God's purposes in the world.

When Jesus chose 12 disciples at the outset of his ministry, he apparently intended to show the continuity between Israel's mission and the one he was about to launch. And after Pentecost the church claimed to be the true Israel, the people of God and heirs of all the promises made to their forebears. First Peter states it clearly: "But you are a chosen race, a royal priesthood, a holy nation, God's own people, that you may declare the wonderful deeds of him who called you out of darkness into his marvelous light" (1 Pet. 2:9).

As the New Testament unfolds and as the life of the church developed, the understanding of God's call was enlarged. Christians came to see that God calls people into the church, that God "calls, gathers and enlightens" them, and that God calls people to different functions within the church, giving them a variety of gifts in the fulfillment of that calling.

How might the concept of the call be viewed in today's church, especially when considering the call to leadership? The call to leadership is, first, a call to a position. While not all leadership functions are carried out by those in the official positions, it is still important to acknowledge that this is the case in organizations of all kinds, including the church. In most churches the pastor is in a leadership position. He or she has met the requirements for the role of leader, and is called, elected, or appointed to assume the responsibilities of the position. Congregations also have numerous positions for lay leadership, chair of the governing board, chair or member of a committee or group. Whatever the exact leadership role or responsibility, it is first of all a position.

Second, the call to leadership is to a relationship, with both other leaders and the people to be led. When one assumes a new position it is wise to learn about the relationships. To whom are you responsible? Who is responsible to you? What aspects of your work need to be approved, and by whom? What must be coordinated, and with whom? Few people work in complete independence, and in our time this is especially true of leaders, most of whom have colleagues and partners. Leaders are members of a team.

Third, the call to leadership is a call to action. The apostles, prophets, and teachers of the early church were called not into honorary positions but to positions of action, with responsibilities to fulfill. The same is true of leadership today. While there is the position of "emeritus" in some organizations, including the church, such is the exception, not the rule. The blunt saying, "Lead, follow, or get out of the way" reflects the fact that leaders are to lead—to initiate and take action, to actually exercise leadership calling. Leaders are those who make things happen that would not otherwise happen. They are people of action.

A MINISTRY

In the present day it is common to speak of a variety of ministries in the church. We still speak of the ministries of preaching, teaching, and pastoral care, but we also speak of youth ministry, of social ministry, of counseling ministry. Congregations have even been known to have bus ministries!

The understanding of ministry needs to be enlarged. We know more clearly than in the past that ministry belongs to the whole people of God. We know too that ministry is service given in the name of Christ, on behalf of or for the well-being of the church and its mission.

Leadership as ministry is not only preparation for ministry; it *is* ministry. Specifically, leadership is ministry:

- When it guides the people of God, helping them fulfill their calling and mission;
- When it organizes the church so that maximum use is made of its resources;

- When it motivates people to affirm and participate in the life of the church.

Leadership is ministry when it works for renewal in the church. In the words of Henri Nouwen: "Christian leadership is called ministry precisely to express that in the service of others new life can be brought about. It is this service which gives eyes to see the flower breaking though the cracks in the street, ears to hear a word of forgiveness muted by hatred and hostility, and hands to feel new life under the cover of death and destruction."[4] The church, too, can grow weary, atrophy, lose both heart and vision. Church leaders minister by calling for repentance, by working for reform and new life.

Leadership in the church is rooted in what we believe about God and the church, the body of the Son, Jesus Christ. The church may have much in common with organizations of various kinds, and it may operate in similar ways, but its beliefs about leadership are rooted deeply in the faith. In the church we believe leadership is one of God's gifts, given for the sake and welfare of the church's life and mission. We believe also that leadership is a calling from God and a ministry through which we serve God.

2

FOR WHAT
PURPOSE?

An ad in the *Wall Street Journal*
said, "People don't want to be managed. They want to be led."

Whoever heard
of a world
manager?
World leader,
yes.
Educational leader.
Political leader
Religious leader.
Scout leader.
Community leader.
Labor leader.
Business leader.
They lead.
They don't manage.
The carrot
always wins
over the stick.
Ask your horse.
You can lead your

horse to water,
but you can't
manage him
to drink.
If you want to
manage somebody,
manage yourself.
Do that well
and you'll
be ready to
stop managing.
And start leading.[1]

To appreciate the role of leadership one need not, however, embrace a negative attitude toward management. While it is helpful to distinguish leadership from management, in actual practice the two activities are often integrated. Indeed, it is often the task of management to implement what leadership has said is the "right thing."

Yet there is something engaging about the statement from the *Wall Street Journal*. Leadership as a subject is more intriguing than management. Leadership can be thought of as an art rather than a science.

In this chapter we consider the overall purpose of leadership, identifying general goals and key functions, and describing two basic leadership types.

Leadership is that which moves persons and organizations toward the fulfillment of their goals. This is a common definition of the subject. What makes leadership in the church difficult, however, is that the church has not one but two overall goals: one that directs attention to the inner life of the church, and another that focuses on the church's outer life. The first has to do with nurturing people in the faith, "to the measure of the stature of the fulness of Christ," as the apostle Paul said it. Today we speak of faith development, of moving through stages of faith, until one reaches the stage called "owned" faith. An ongoing goal of the church is therefore to evoke and nurture faith in the lives of its people.

The second goal turns our attention away from ourselves and toward others, toward the world at large, with ministries of evangelism, outreach, and service. Not only are we to grow up to maturity in the faith ourselves, we are to make disciples of all nations; we are to be the salt of the earth and the light of the world. The second goal therefore calls the church to look beyond itself to the world it seeks to serve.

Leadership in the church helps the church move toward the fulfillment of both goals; thus leadership challenges are greater in the church than in most organizations.

KEY LEADERSHIP FUNCTIONS

If leadership exists to move persons and groups toward the fulfillment of their goals, an appropriate question is, What are the key functions of leadership? The question pertains here to the larger functions, not the day-to-day tasks considered in more detail in chapters 11-14. Functions, as the term is used here, refers to the continuing leadership responsibilities in organizations of various kinds. Consider six key functions.

First, clarify and maintain the vision. "Where there is no vision, the people perish," said the writer of Proverbs (29:18; KJV). This is true in our personal lives as we experience the listlessness that comes from having no goals or plans for the future, and it is true in the life of organizations. When Warren Bennis and Burt Nanus studied 90 top leaders they discovered a common denominator: they all had a compelling vision, a dream about their work.[2]

To clarify the vision for the church we begin with what the Scripture sets forth as God's vision for the world. We appropriately ask, What is God's will for the world? What is God doing with his global family, and where is he leading it? What does it mean that God wills for all to be saved and come to the knowledge of the truth? It is important for the leadership of the church and of individual congregations to clarify its understanding of the Scripture's vision.

Then, clarify how your congregation can participate in the pursuit of that vision and, in doing so, develop its own vision. Ask,

What aspect of the larger vision is ours to pursue? What do we do in our time and place? How do we proceed? This subject is pursued in greater depth in chapter 11. Here let it be noted that visioning for the future is one of the key functions of leadership.

Second, affirm the values of the organization. "A community lives in the minds of its members," writes John Gardner, "in shared assumptions, beliefs, customs, ideas that give meaning, ideas that motivate. And among the ideas are norms or values. In any healthy and reasonably coherent community, people come to have shared views concerning right and wrong, better and worse—in personal conduct, in governing, in art, whatever."[3] This is especially true in the church, a value-oriented organization. It is especially significant for church leadership to affirm the values of the church: love, justice, truth, and peace.

When lay persons are commissioned for leadership in congregations of the Evangelical Church in America, for example, they are given these words of exhortation:

> You are to see that the words and deeds of this household of faith reflect him in whose name we gather. You are to be examples of faith active in love, to help maintain the life and harmony of this congregation.

This statement calls for affirmation of the church's values.

The third key function of leadership is to symbolize the standards and expectations of the organization. While this is similar to affirming the organization's values, it is less direct and more subtle. Leadership must be transparent to be effective; it must be a personification of the organization's vision and commitments. The man who becomes a foreman is set apart from his former coworkers in subtle ways; he is now a symbol of management. The corporate woman symbolizes the corporation for which she works. The noncommissioned officer symbolizes the military chain of command. The pastor and the elected leaders of the congregation symbolize the church. Writes John Gardner:

> Most leaders become quite aware of the symbolic aspects of their role and make effective use of them. One of the 20th century leaders

29

who did so most skillfully was Gandhi. In the issues he chose to do battle on, in the way he conducted his campaigns, in the jail terms and the fasting, in his manner of dress, he symbolized his people, their desperate need and their struggle against oppression.[4]

In the church, leaders assume roles that are sometimes prophetic and sometimes priestly—that is, sometimes challenging and sometimes comforting. Leaders in the prophetic role seek to stir the followers out of their lethargy and complacency. At other times, now in the priestly role, leaders seek to reassure and give comfort. In either case, however, the function symbolizes the church's values and commitments.

The fourth key leadership function has to do with maintenance of the organization, seeing that it is provided for. In smaller organizations the leaders are also the doers, practicing hands-on management. They are the actual maintainers of the organization. This is often the case in small churches where the pastor and elected leaders actually operate the church.

In larger churches the pastor and elected leaders are often in supervisory roles. They have overall responsibility for the life of the congregation, but much of the work is delegated to others. In this way they fulfill the fourth leadership responsibility, maintaining the organization.

The fifth leadership function is service to the organization. Robert Greenleaf holds together two concepts that seem to be contradictory: servant and leader. His central idea is that the leader who is legitimate, powerful, and great is first and last a servant. There are other ingredients for effective leadership, says Greenleaf, but service is basic.

Leadership serves the organization, helping it, in turn, to be an organization that serves. Through service, all who are touched by it become "healthier, wiser, freer, more autonomous, more likely themselves to become servants."[5]

Included in Greenleaf's concept of servanthood is the conviction that servant leaders are not merely servants of what is, but shapers of what might be. Servant leaders help clarify and pursue

30

the vision of the organization and then they work toward the fulfillment of that vision.

The sixth and final key function of leadership has to do with the institution's renewal, an ongoing function in organizations of all kinds. To live is to change; to live well is to change often—not merely for the sake of change, but for the sake of the mission. Sometimes, of course, leadership must preserve and conserve. Not all change or proposed change is for the good. Yet because of our rapidly changing world, to forgo change is not a live option. At times the only options are to change or to die.

The biblical perspective acknowledges the tendency of all things—the whole creation and all of its institutions, including the church—to deteriorate and decay. The Bible therefore calls for change, for repentance and renewal, offering the promise of new life. Working for renewal is a key function of leadership.

TWO BASIC TYPES OF LEADERSHIP

In his book on leadership, James MacGregor Burns, historian and political scientist, identifies two different kinds of leadership: transactional and transforming.

> The relations of most leaders and followers are transactional— leaders approach followers with an eye to exchanging one thing for another: jobs for votes or subsidies for campaign contributions. Such transactions comprise the bulk of the relationship among leaders and followers. . . . Transforming leadership, while more complex is more potent. The transforming leader recognizes and exploits an existing need or demand of a potential follower. But, beyond that, the transforming leader looks for potential motives in followers, seeks to satisfy higher needs, and engages the full person of the follower. The result of transforming leadership is a relation- ship of mutual stimulation and elevation that converts followers into leaders and may convert leaders into moral agents.[6]

According to Burns, transactional leaders give their followers something they want in exchange for something that they, the leaders, want—a barter of sorts. In the life of an organization, for example, transactional leaders are those who manage the affairs, keep the wheels turning and the machinery in good repair, resulting in an organizational life that is efficient and comparatively peaceful. Every organization needs transactional leaders, or, at least, leaders willing to do the work of transactional leaders.

Burns's second type of leader, the transforming leader, is more of a motivator than a keeper of the status quo, more of a change agent than a caretaker. Transforming leaders, says Burns, are able to raise others to higher levels of motivation and morality. Burns notes that some definitions of leadership see leaders making followers do what leaders want them to do. In contrast, he states: "I define leadership as leaders inducing followers to act for certain goals that represent the values and the motivations . . . the aspirations and expectations of both leaders and followers. And the genius of leadership lies in the manner in which leaders see and act on their own and their followers' values and motivations."[7]

The transforming style of leadership has significant precedence in the church, for both the Old Testament prophets and Jesus were often in that role. The prophets called for repentance and new life, appealing to their hearer's identity as people of God, who were called to be a blessing to the nations of the world. When Jesus declared, "You have heard it said . . . but I say unto you," he clearly called for renewal and change, a higher level of morality and faithfulness. In his book *Christ and Culture*, H. Richard Niebuhr supports this view by referring to St. John's Gospel and the writings of St. Augustine. Christ redirects, renews, and regenerates the life of the world, says Niebuhr. He is properly seen as a transforming leader.

While leaders in today's church must necessarily be transactional much of the time, overseeing and managing its everyday affairs, they dare not neglect the role of the transforming leader, affirming and articulating the biblical vision for the world, calling for faithfulness, and encouraging the work of renewal.

The servant-leader of Robert Greenleaf may be seen as an example of the transforming leader. To be effective, says Greenleaf, the leader must be a servant. He or she cannot be the aloof boss, but a *primus inter pares* (first among equals) who builds a team and who is able and willing to listen, heal, conceptualize, dream, unify, and implement. "This is my thesis," says Greenleaf, "caring for persons, the more able and the less able serving each other . . . the rock upon which a good society is built."[8]

Greenleaf does not confine his views to the church or educational institutions, places where they would seem quite acceptable. Rather, he believes they are appropriate for institutions of all kinds, including business organizations.

> When the business manager who is fully committed to this ethic is asked, "What are you in business for?" the answer may be: "I am in the business of growing people—people who are stronger, healthier, more autonomous, more self-reliant, more competent. Incidentally, we also make and sell at a profit things that people want to buy so we can pay for all this. We play that game hard and well and we are successful by the usual standards, but that is really incidental. I recall a time when there was a complaint about manipulation. We don't hear it anymore. We manage the business about the same way we always did. We simply changed our aim."[9]

In the church, however, the servant-leader style is most fitting, says Greenleaf. Jesus took the form of a servant, stating, "Whoever would be great among you must be your servant, and whoever would be first among you must be your slave; even as the Son of man came not to be served but to serve, and to give his life as a ransom for many" (Matt. 20:27-28).

With that in mind Greenleaf addresses the church as follows:

> We need a religion, and a church to husband its service, to heal the pervasive alienation and become a major building force in a new society that is more just and more loving, and that provides greater creative opportunities for its people.[10]

Greenleaf goes on to speak of a "growing edge" church, a church that would live up to its opportunities in our world.

> The first task of the growing edge church is to learn what neither Luther nor Fox knew: how to build a society of equals in which

there is a strong lay leadership and a trustee board with a chairman functioning as *primus inter pares*, and with the pastor functioning as a *primus inter pares* for the many who do the work of the church.[11]

The second task is to make of the church a powerful force to build leadership strength in those persons who have the opportunity to lead in other institutions, and give them constant support.[12]

While the overall purpose of leadership is to move people and organizations toward the fulfillment of their goals, the actual functions of leaders are many—to clarify vision, to affirm values, to symbolize standards and expectations; to maintain, serve, and renew the organization. The responsibilities are sometimes carried out in transactional ways and sometimes in transforming ways, but the latter seems especially appropriate in the church, and is particularly adaptable to Robert Greenleaf's concept of the servant-leader.

3

THE MAKING
OF
LEADERS

There are many kinds of leaders. Some are natural leaders, "born leaders," having the personality and skills that equip them for the role and responsibilities of leadership. Others have learned how to be leaders. They have read, studied, practiced. To them the gift of leadership is a capacity to be honed and perfected; it is a learned art, not a natural skill. They are made, not born.

Leaders reflect an amazing variety of qualities and personalities. Churchill is remembered for his ideas and rhetorical powers; Gandhi for his vision and commitment; Lenin for his ideas and determination; Florence Nightingale for her compassion and assertiveness. Even among leaders in the same field there are significant differences. In the military, for example, George Marshall was low-keyed and self-effacing, Douglas MacArthur was flamboyant, Dwight Eisenhower was an outstanding coalition builder. The biblical record depicts a feisty apostle Paul, concerned about right understanding and right living; a mild apostle John, concerned about loving relationships; a planner and organizer in the person of Nehemiah, concerned with getting the job done.

The variety of leaders raises questions about the nature of leadership and leadership style. Are leaders born or are they made? Are there qualities of leadership that are effective in a variety of settings, qualities that should be held up as models? And what about the various styles of leadership? These are among the issues we consider in this chapter.

THREE APPROACHES

The three general approaches to the subject of leadership qualities and style reflect the three general periods of research and study: the trait period from the turn of the century to the early 1940s; the behavioral period from the early 1940s into the 1960s; and the situational period from the 1960s to the present.[1] These three approaches serve as the basis of our exploration of the subject.

Traits

Still common is the idea that leaders are born, not made. Of course, such was literally the case in the past. When people were born to rank and wealth, they assumed leadership responsibilities whether they had the qualifications or not. Today, however, when we say leaders are born we usually refer to their personality traits. Max Weber borrowed the term "charisma" from the church historian Rudolph Sohm who had in turn borrowed it from St. Paul, and used it to describe persons with exceptional powers or qualities. While St. Paul had used the term to refer to manifestations of God's grace, Weber gave it his own interpretation, seeing "charisma" as a special quality of personality, endowing a person with unique abilities. The word "charismatic" is part of the vocabulary of our time and is often used to describe the leader who has exceptional ability to elicit emotional responses from followers.

While research rejects the older view that held that there are certain inborn traits that equip one for leadership, many students of the subject would still point to qualities and characteristics that seem to enhance leadership ability. University professor Edward

36

Wynne lists characteristics of leaders that reflect a combination of skills and attitudes:

- The insight to understand the thoughts and values underlying the thinking of significant persons and groups;
- The judgment to determine which issues can become sources of potential group coalescence;
- The moral qualities to decide whether such issues are deserving of concern;
- The desire to unite people around such issues;
- The ability to commit oneself to such an end over long periods of time;
- The communication and interpersonal skill to foster cooperation;
- The sense of acquiescence necessary to loyally serve others who may grant the authority to lead.[2]

Some people may have one or more of the characteristics innately; others may have them as a result of their overall life's experience; still others as the result of intentional development and education. The traits are thus learned and practiced consciously and deliberatively.

In her book *Real Power*, Janet Hagberg writes about various stages of personal power in ways that also refer to leadership characteristics and traits. Hagberg refers to six different stages of power, which are, in a sense, stages of growth in maturity and, in another sense, stages of leadership trait development. She then makes suggestions for ways to move to a higher stage.[3]

Stage one, the stage of powerlessness, is marked by low self-esteem, low skill development, and a general lack of knowledge about the requirements of the job. This person can move to a higher stage by building self-esteem, developing skills, and gaining information.

Stage two, the stage of association, is marked by a dependence on the supervisor while he or she learns the culture of the organization. A person in this stage may still lack confidence and have a need for security, but can move to the next stage by developing competencies, taking risks, earning the necessary credentials.

Stage three is marked by symbols. "People at Stage Three are in the thick of things," writes Hagberg. "They have striven for degrees or positions or salary levels or sports cars or homes in the suburbs or luxury vacations, and now they have attained them."[4] But the satisfactions in stage three are not lasting, and persons in it begin to look for the credibility and respect of the next stage. Reflection and self-examination can help one prepare for the next stage.

Stage four, "Power by Reflection," has the characteristics of strength and competence. Persons in this stage are reflective about themselves, skilled at monitoring, and comfortable with their personal style. As Hagberg describes them: "Fours have a solid reputation of honesty, fairness, sound judgement, and follow-through—in a word, integrity."[5] In Hagberg's view, stage four is the first stage that can be considered true leadership, since the first three depend in one way or another on position power. To move to the next stage it is necessary to forgive others, to have long silent times, to experience loss, and let go.

Persons in stage five are hard to spot, says Hagberg, because they don't care if they are ever spotted. Stage five people are self-accepting and calm; they are humble, visionary, generous in empowering others, confident about life's purpose, and usually aware of a spiritual dimension to life. Persons in stage five, however, may be held back by a lack of faith or by unwillingness to give up what they have spent so much time and energy accumulating: reputation, possessions, knowledge. According to Hagberg, they can move ahead only in individual ways.

Stage six, called "Gestalt," is often perceived as being above the battle of life, above the normal, everyday concerns. Persons in this stage would be the proverbial absentminded professor—or would at least act like one. Sometimes they seem aloof and lost in their own thoughts. But the times of reflection and solitude are times of refueling and recharging—times that empower the stage six person to be available to others. Stage six people are comfortable with paradox, unafraid of death, satisfied with quiet lives of service. They are held back only by their human constraints.

As Hagberg points out, most people tend to fluctuate between the six stages, not remaining in any one of them permanently. Yet by honest reflection and intentional effort one can move from the lower stage to the higher, and begin to exhibit the qualities of the higher stages. Hagberg notes that one can be a leader at any of the stages but one cannot be a true leader until stage four is reached—"Power by Reflection." Hagberg lists major characteristics of those she calls true leaders:

- Follow a vision, a purpose, an ideal;
- Allow for win-win, not just win-lose;
- Empower others, not themselves;
- Have balance in life between work, community, and family;
- Can be vulnerable and reflective;
- Treat women, men, and minorities as equals; Ask why, not how;
- Have a spiritual connection to power within and beyond;
- See the bottom line as a means to a larger organizational purpose, not an end in itself;
- Live with integrity as their hallmark.[6]

While it is usually mistaken to speak of born leaders, implying that some are born with the qualities of leadership, it is nevertheless useful to identify leadership traits, to think and speak of them and to hold them up as goals or "north stars" to elicit our growth and development. Hagberg's stages serve that purpose.

Behavioral

Our review of the trait theory has moved us toward the second way of understanding the nature and basis of leadership, namely, the behavioral. People are not born leaders, says this view which was studied and emphasized especially in the 1940s and into the 1960s. Rather, people lead by acting in identifiable "styles."

Two Basic Orientations. Those who study the behavioral aspects of leadership point out that while there are several different styles there are only two basic orientations: we are either task-oriented or people-oriented. The task-oriented person emphasizes getting the job done, while the one who is person-oriented is more concerned with relationships. No one is completely one way or the other, and people commonly fluctuate between the two, sometimes intuitively, sometimes intentionally. Yet it seems that we are basically one or the other.

Robert Blake and Jane Mouton diagram the typical tension between task accomplishment and the development of personal relationships in what they call the "Managerial Grid"[R] (Figure 1).[7]

The horizontal line shows concern for production. A leader with a rating of nine on the horizontal line has a maximum concern for production. The vertical line shows concern for relationships, and a leader with a nine on this line has a maximum concern for interpersonal relationships. The ideal leadership orientation would be a nine, nine—an impossible goal to achieve, perhaps, but worth thinking about nevertheless.

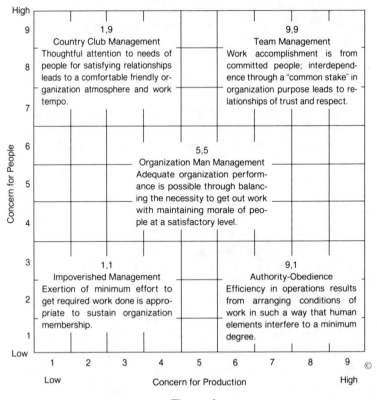

Figure 1

To get a quick reading on your own orientation try the checklist below.[8] (Instructions: Identify the person in your group that you work with least well. Imagine the two of you working together. Rate yourself on the following characteristics. Circle the appropriate numbers and record them in the blanks at the right.)

Pleasant	8	7	6	5	4	3	2	1	Unpleasant	_____
Gentle	8	7	6	5	4	3	2	1	Hostile	_____
Rebellious	8	7	6	5	4	3	2	1	Cooperative	_____
Open	8	7	6	5	4	3	2	1	Closed	_____
Nasty	8	7	6	5	4	3	2	1	Nice	_____
Insecure	8	7	6	5	4	3	2	1	Self-confident	_____
Hard Working	8	7	6	5	4	3	2	1	Lazy	_____
Abrasive	8	7	6	5	4	3	2	1	Friendly	_____
Negative	8	7	6	5	4	3	2	1	Positive	_____
Trustworthy	8	7	6	5	4	3	2	1	Untrustworthy	_____

(After totaling your score turn to the end of the chapter for the interpretation.)

Your orientation—whether person- or task-oriented—is an expression of your personality. If you are energized by people contacts, are sociable and outgoing, you are most likely a person-oriented leader. But if you find your deepest satisfactions in goal achievement, your greatest rewards in accomplishing tasks, you are a task-oriented person. Which is best? Which is most suitable and effective for work in the church? When we consider the ministry of Jesus we realize that we need both orientations. Jesus' message, of course, was one of high relationships. He attracted the masses; he exhibited grace and compassion; he said, "This I command you, to love one another" (John 15:17). In another sense, Jesus was task-oriented, concerned about the accomplishment of his Father's work: "I glorified thee on earth, having accomplished the work which thou gavest me to do" (John 17:4). He seemed driven to his task: "We must work the works of him who sent me, while it is day; night comes when no man can work"

(John 9:4). His exhortation to his followers was one of work: "Go therefore and make disciples of all nations, baptizing . . . and teaching . . . " (Matt. 28:19, 20).

Jesus was able to integrate the two orientations; he could be effectively task-oriented or person-oriented according to the situation at hand and his purpose at the time.

As indicated, the orientation we choose is an expression of our own personalities. It is also an expression of our understanding of human nature. This is clarified by Lyle Schaller (see Figure 2).

The first division is between the leader who sees most people to be active, self-actualizing, and self-motivating (1), and the leader who sees them as passive except for responding to the environment and external stimuli (2). Next, note the subdivision of the leaders in the first category. This division is between the leader who sees people as good, operating under the assumption that they will do the good and the right whenever possible (1a), and the leader who acts on the assumption that people are bad and in need of restraint (1b). The Christian understanding of human nature is that people are both good and evil, made in God's image yet fallen and sinful. The Christian view is represented by the box enclosed with the dotted line in the diagram (1b).

The style of the leaders is reflected by the arrows in the diagram. The leader who believes people are active and good will follow the style represented by arrow A. This leader's efforts

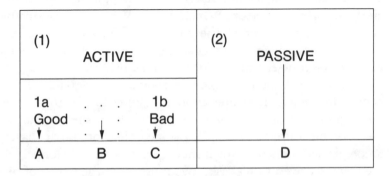

Figure 2

will be directed toward removing barriers. The leader who believes people are active but inclined toward evil will choose the style represented by arrow C, and will give attention to rules, regulations, and prohibitions. The leader who believes people are a mixture of good and evil will develop a style represented by B—working sometimes to increase freedom and sometimes to restrict it. The leader who sees people as passive but responsive to external stimuli will adopt the style represented by arrow D, employing the positive and negative reinforcements of reward and punishment.

Three Basic Styles. In addition to the two basic orientations—task and relationship—it is helpful to understand the three basic leadership styles: authoritarian, laissez-faire, and participative. While again it should be noted that our understanding of human nature as well as our experience in life will influence our leadership style, most people are flexible enough to alter their styles as circumstances change.

The authoritarian style is one in which the leader prefers to make the decisions and direct the implementation of the plan without the participation of others. An authoritarian leader may consult with others and even work for a consensus, but few votes are taken. The authoritarian leader makes most of the decisions and announces them as he or she sees fit. This leader is usually seen as strong and decisive.

Figure 3, adapted from one by Robert Tannebaum and Warren Schmidt,[10] illustrates the leadership style continuum, ranging from the authoritarian on the far left to the laissez-faire on the far right.

The laissez-faire style, depicted on the diagram at the far right and as expressed in real life, is practically no leadership at all. Leaders of this style wait for the group to initiate and decide, offering little if any perspective or information, seldom if ever making suggestions or recommendations. They would typically be seen as "weak" or "poor" leaders.

The third of the three basic styles, the participative, is between the two extremes, and provides for flexibility to move up and down the continuum as the particular situation requires. As the

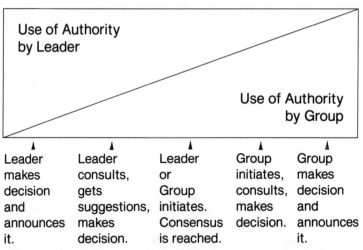

Leader	Leader	Leader	Group	Group
makes	consults,	or	initiates,	makes
decision	gets	Group	consults,	decision
and	suggestions,	initiates.	makes	and
announces	makes	Consensus	decision.	announces
it.	decision.	is reached.		it.

Reprinted by permission of *Harvard Business Review*. An exhibit from "How to Choose a Leadership Pattern" by Robert Tannebaum and Warren H. Schmidt, May/June 1973. Copyright © 1973 by the President and Fellows of Harvard College; all rights reserved.

Figure 3

name suggests, this style invites and welcomes the participation of others in the decision-making process. A shortcoming of this style is inefficiency, since time consumed often far exceeds the importance of the matter at hand. However, there are many advantages to the participatory style, for example:

- People have a chance to express their views.
- More ideas and perspectives are considered.
- The leader is free to be more forthright.
- Motivation to implement decisions is usually greater following participation.

John Clemens and Douglas Mayer point out in their book *The Classic Touch* that John Stuart Mill, who lived from 1806 to 1873, made a strong case for participative leadership more than 100 years ago. Mill stated three reasons for his opinion:

First, if any opinion is compelled to silence, that opinion may, for aught we can certainly know, be true. To deny this is to assume our own infallibility.

Second, though the silenced opinion may be in error, it may, and very commonly does, contain a portion of truth. . . . It is only by

44

the collision of adverse opinions that the remainder of the truth has any chance of being supplied.

Thirdly, even if the received opinion be not only true, but the whole truth, unless it is . . . vigorously and earnestly contested, it will, by most of those who receive it, be held in the manner of a prejudice, with little comprehension or feeling of its rational grounds.[11]

Is there a best style of leadership? The research indicates that there is not a style that is best under all circumstances. Sometimes it is best for the leader to exercise the authority of his or her position and be simply authoritarian: Let's do it this way. At other times it is best for the leader to take the laissez-faire approach, when simply waiting may be the best decision. At still other times the participatory style is the best, when the subject at hand is of such importance that the opinion and voice of many is desirable, or when the morale is such that it would be enhanced by the participatory style of leadership and government. While there is no style that is best under all circumstances, the participatory style is especially appropriate in the church, for it expresses what the church believes about the priesthood of all believers.

Situational

Leadership style, while discussed under the general heading of the behavioral view of leadership, cannot be confined to that category. As indicated, the focus of most leadership research since the 1960s has been on the situational approach to the subject. Many of the insights gained during this time have reshaped the understanding of the behavioral perspective, which is why our discussion of the situational approach will seem like an extension of the behavioral view. The situationists also speak of person-oriented and task-oriented leaders. They, too, speak of various styles of leadership, noting with the behaviorists that the style to use at a given moment is dependent upon the particular circumstances.

Paul Hersey, a popular writer on situational leadership, notes that a leader's success "depends upon the interaction among the leader, follower, boss, associates, organization, job demands, and time constraints"[12]—factors that tend to be present in the environment at any particular time. Hersey goes on to point out how each of the factors can influence the whole picture.

Leader: The leader brings his or her style and attitude to the situation.

Follower: Followers also bring their attitudes and behavior to the situation, both individually and collectively.

Boss: Everybody is accountable to someone, if not to an individual then to a group. The boss has expectations.

Associates: These are the organizational peers whose cooperation is needed.

Organizations: Every organization has a culture and a way of doing things.

Job Demands: This refers to the followers' perception of the work and implies the amount and kind of supervision.

Time: This influences the style of the leader, for the shorter the decision time, the more directive the leader will have to be.

Of all the variables, there is one that is crucial, says Hersey, "the relationship between the leader and the follower. If the follower decides not to follow, the other variables become unimportant."[13]

Kenneth Blanchard has also popularized and applied many of the basic insights of situational leadership, especially in his book, *Leadership and the One Minute Manager*. Blanchard sees four basic leadership styles: directing, coaching, supporting, and delegating.

In the *directing* mode the leader provides specific instructions and close supervision.

In the *coaching* mode the leader continues to give direction and supervision but also explains decisions, invites suggestions, and notes progress.

In the *supporting* style the leader facilitates and gives support, and begins to share decision-making responsibilities.

In the *delegating* mode the leader turns over the decision making and problem solving to coworkers. See Figure 4[14].

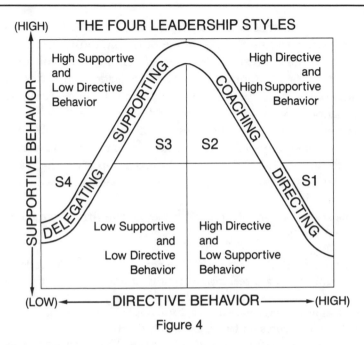

Figure 4

How does the leader decide which style to use? Blanchard says that it is determined by the development level of the follower, the follower's competence and commitment, ranging in each case from low to high to variable.

Directing Style is for people who lack competence but are enthusiastic and committed.

Coaching Style is for people who have some competence but lack commitment.

Supporting Style is for people who have competence but lack confidence or motivation.

Delegating Style is for people who have both competence and commitment.[15]

A More Simple Approach. With the help of Lyle Schaller it is possible to clarify and affirm a more simple approach, a leadership style that will serve well under a variety of circumstances. After tracing through some of the literature on the subject, and in the context of his experience as a church consultant, Schaller states: "Countless variations in leadership styles exist because of the many facets of leadership and the huge variation in personalities, skills, gifts, talents, and experience."[16] The variations are so many, as Schaller sees it, that one is better off finding a more simple approach—which he then proposes. Overriding the differences and variations "is a leadership style that can be learned, that is compatible with a variety of personalities, and that fits most roles."[17]

This style consists of two components, the first of which is to affirm and build:

> In simple terms that means that the person following this style of leadership is always seeking to identify and affirm strengths, resources, and assets and to build on these strengths in raising or discussing specific issues. This approach is in sharp contrast to the leader who focuses on faults, problems, shortcomings, limitations, weaknesses, imperfections, and deficiencies. The leader who seeks to affirm and build usually is tremendously impressed and awed by God's goodness, by His creation, by His glory, by His forgiveness of human failings, by His generosity, and by His limitless love.[18]

The second component of Schaller's proposed leadership style is the willingness and ability to intervene in the life of the group. According to Schaller there are at least three different ways of making a constructive intervention.

One: Ask questions. Do so from the context of the group's purpose and goals.

Two: Redefine the issue or revise the agenda so that the group doesn't end up talking only about symptoms.

Three: Give people a chance to talk themselves into a new view of the situation before asking them to make a decision.

Affirm and intervene, says Schaller, by way of summary. Affirm the good and the positive. Look for strengths and assets, and build on them. Also be willing to intervene with questions, observations and suggestions, and with a proper sense of timing.[19]

Few leaders, if any, are born. Most effective leaders are products of education, perseverance, and practice. Leadership is a skill, an art to be learned and practiced. It is usually the result of intentional effort.

In the next chapter we consider three areas of knowledge that are important for leaders: they need to know themselves, know the people they lead, and know the dynamics of power.

Note: Here is the key to the checklist on page 41. Total your points by adding the column of numbers. A score of 46 points or more suggests that you tend to be a relationship-motivated leader. Forty-five points or less suggests a task-motivated leader. The more extreme the score, the greater the orientation.

PART TWO

WHAT
LEADERS NEED
TO KNOW

We must learn common leadership principles, but power is released as we become true to our God-given personalities.

Harold Myra

The personal authenticity of the minister, priest or rabbi is the greatest strength of any congregation. The inauthenticity of the clergy is the greatest weakness of organized religion.

John Harris

Now you are the body of Christ and individually members of it.

1 Cor. 12:27

All things should be done decently and in order.

1 Cor. 14:40

4

LEADER:
KNOW YOURSELF

One of the reasons leadership is such a complex subject is the fact that there are many variables. Douglas McGregor writes in *The Human Side of Enterprise* that every organization has at least four: the characteristics of the leader, the characteristics of the followers, the characteristics of the organization, and the general social and political milieu.[1] In this chapter we consider the first two of McGregor's variables, focusing on the characteristics of the leaders and the followers, emphasizing especially how leaders can gain greater awareness of themselves.

While in the church we believe that God knows us—knows "when I sit down and when I rise up," knows "my thoughts from afar"—we believe that our leadership effectiveness is strengthened through an increase of self- and other-awareness. "The effective leader must know himself, his talents and limitations," states Michael Maccoby, following an in-depth study of six particular leaders in the United States and Europe.[2] Edwin Friedman, Jewish rabbi and family systems therapist, talks about the importance of self-definition and self-differentiation. "The overall health and functioning of any organization depend primarily on one or two people at the top," writes Friedman, and the key to successful leadership, including effective spiritual leadership, "has more to do with the leader's capacity for self-definition than with the ability to motivate others."[3]

What Friedman means by self-definition or self-differentiation is essentially what we more commonly speak of as self-awareness or self-understanding, including the ability to articulate to others what that is. A leader's personal characteristics and qualities influence his or her effectiveness, for good or for ill. The ill effects can be reduced and the good effects increased through self-understanding.

WAYS OF KNOWING YOURSELF

One of the saddest lines in Arthur Miller's play *The Death of a Salesman* is spoken by Biff as the family stands by the side of the grave following the burial of Willy Lohman: "Dad never knew who he was." Fortunately, there are ways of increasing our self-awareness, and in this chapter we identify and describe some of them.

Reading Self-Help Books

Not everyone can readily go off to seminars and workshops, much less undergo psychological testing. But many who conduct seminars also write books, and reading and reflecting on some of their works can have positive results. Some examples are: *The Art of Understanding Yourself* by Cecil Osborne (Grand Rapids, Mich.: Zondervan, 1967); *Why Am I Afraid To Tell You Who I Am?* and *Why Am I Afraid To Love?* by John Powell (Niles, Ill.: Argus, 1969, 1972); *Gifts Differing* by Isabel Myers (Palo Alto, Calif.: Consulting Psychologists Press, 1980); *Confidence* by Alan Loy McGinnis (Minneapolis: Augsburg, 1987); and *God's Gifted People* by Gary L. Harbaugh (Minneapolis: Augsburg, 1988). Studies of greater depth are *On Being Human* by Ray S. Anderson (Grand Rapids, Mich.: Wm. B. Eerdmans, 1982); *Seven Theories of Human Nature* by Leslie Stevenson (New York: Oxford, 1987); and *Pastor As Person* by Gary L. Harbaugh (Minneapolis: Augsburg, 1984).

Clinical Pastoral Education

A more concentrated way of increasing self-understanding, especially for pastors and seminary students, is Clinical Pastoral Education (C.P.E.). Most often conducted in a hospital setting, C.P.E. programs seek to enhance the person's effectiveness in ministry, especially one-on-one and counseling ministries, as he or she learns more about human dynamics. Those involved in C.P.E. programs also learn about themselves, and through reflection and feedback from supervisors and peers they begin to identify barriers that prohibit effective ministry and discover ways of overcoming those barriers.

Psychological Testing

Still another way to increase self-awareness is through various kinds of psychological testing. When Michael Maccoby made his study of leaders, his two main tools were a 50-question interview guide and the Rorschach test. While acknowledging that the Rorschach is not foolproof, Maccoby believes it nevertheless is helpful in showing a person's cognitive style and temperament, demonstrating how leadership style is an expression of temperament and character. The Rorschach test gives an indication of how a person approaches new experiences, a person's emotional responses, feelings about intimacy, and degree of aggressiveness.[4]

The Jo-Hari Window

Psychologists Joseph Luft and Harry Ingram designed a tool for use in small groups that can help the members of the group deepen their self-awareness, especially as the result of getting feedback from the others in the group.

The Jo-Hari window has four "panes," each with a particular label (Figure 5)[5].

The arena is the clear pane of glass through which you can see yourself and through which others can see you. It reveals what you know about yourself and what others know about you.

The blind spot is like a one-way glass. You cannot see through

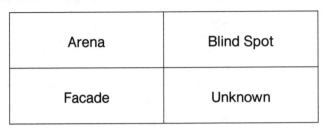

Figure 5

it, but others can from their side, which means they can see things about you that you don't see yourself.

The facade is also a one-way glass, but turned the opposite direction so that through it you can see things about yourself that others don't see, usually because you don't want them to see.

The unknown is like a frosted pane of glass, indicating that there are some things about yourself that neither you nor anyone else knows anything about.

How is a Jo-Hari window used? If trust in a group or with another person is high, it can be used to enlarge the arena pane and reduce the size of the others as more of the self is revealed and a greater self-awareness is achieved. When we have the necessary trust, we can solicit feedback from others on our leadership style, for example, and in that way learn more about ourselves. It is probably unrealistic (and undesirable) to think that the blind spot, facade, and unknown panes can be entirely eliminated, for we will never know ourselves completely. Yet leadership effectiveness is enhanced when the arena pane on the Jo-Hari window is enlarged in proportion to the others. Others will have to make fewer guesses about where the leader stands on particular issues, reducing the chances for misinterpretation or misunderstanding. Also, when used in a leadership group, the Jo-Hari window can lead to more open communication.

The Awareness Wheel

Another tool that is useful for increasing self-awareness is the Awareness Wheel, a tool designed for use with the Couple

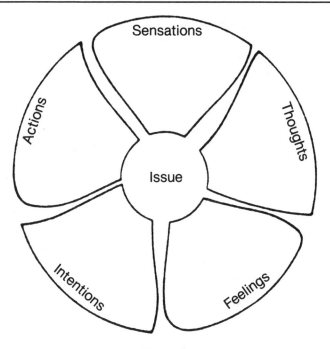

Figure 6

Communication program.[6] A basic assumption of this program is that communication is strengthened when the parties involved have reasonably accurate awareness of themselves—their feelings, thoughts, and intentions. As shown in Figure 6, the wheel has five components: sensations, thoughts, feelings, intentions, and actions.

"Sensations" represents what you receive through your five senses—the channel through which all information comes to you.

"Thoughts" represents the interpretation you give to what you sense. For example, when you see (through the sense of sight) that another person is frowning, you would conclude (through thinking and interpretation) that he or she is worried or angry, or at least unhappy.

Your interpretation, often made intuitively, leads to the third component of the Awareness Wheel—"Feelings." These are the result of how you interpret or what you think about what you have received through your senses. Feelings are often mixed, and they come in varying degrees. Your feelings in response to the frowning person may be fear, pity, or concern—or a combination of the three.

"Intentions" refers to what you intend to do in the given situation. It represents your plan, possibly long-range, possibly short-range, sometimes made deliberately and sometimes spontaneously. In response to the frowning person you may decide to go on your way, or to stop and inquire if there is something you can do.

The fifth part of the Awareness Wheel, "Actions," refers to what you actually do in a given situation. While your intentions are your plans, your actions represent a definite commitment to act. They also reveal some things about yourself and they are what other people see and respond to. It can be helpful to take a look at your patterns of action. Being aware of them will help you change them, when appropriate, and will tell you why people respond to you the way they do.

Your Awareness Wheel is always about a specific subject. This fact is represented by the sixth part of the wheel, the hub, here called the "Issue." This indicates that our awareness always revolves around an issue of some kind, a situation to face or a decision to make. In our example, the frowning person is the issue about whom we consciously or unconsciously exercise our Awareness Wheel. Using the wheel intentionally can increase our ability to understand others as well as ourselves.

Myers-Briggs Type Indicator

To understand the Myers-Briggs approach to self-awareness, it is helpful to know that it is based on the insights of Carl Jung, the Swiss psychiatrist who developed the theory that personality differences are usually found in patterns. These patterns, consisting of four pairs of personality traits, are reflections of our unique temperaments and gifts and of how they have developed. A combination of patterns—a possibility of 16 in all—reflects our personality type.

According to Jung's theory, the first pattern distinguishes two different ways of viewing the world. Extroverts focus their attention on the outside world of actions and persons; introverts look inward, giving attention to ideas and concepts.

The second pair of personality characteristics addresses the question of how persons perceive the world—through the senses, paying attention to the immediate and real facts of life, or through the use of intuition, which notes not so much the specific things as the whole. The intuitive type sees the forest, the sensing type sees the trees.

The third pattern relates to how we make decisions—by thinking or by feeling. Do we consider things objectively, rationally thinking our way through a situation or problem? If so, we are obviously a thinking type. If we prefer to go more by our feelings, subjectively weighing the values and choices, we are a feeling type.

There is a fourth pair of opposites, measuring how a person tends to live—in a decisive, orderly, and planned way, or in a spontaneous and flexible way that more easily adapts to life. The words to describe this category of differences are judging (not judgmental) and perceptive.

It should be pointed out that Jung did not say that a person is confined to one or the other of these opposite traits. Rather, a person can be somewhat extroverted and somewhat introverted, somewhat thinking and somewhat feeling. It is a matter of degree, of inclination or tendency.

Jung believed that these tendencies develop and become stronger through use. For example, those who use their feelings become more feeling in the process, and those who choose the rational approach become more rational as time goes on. By the same token, the qualities that are not used tend to weaken further, like a muscle that goes unused.

The Myers-Briggs Type Indicator (MBTI), developed by Katharine Briggs and Isabel Briggs Myers, illustrates how different combinations of the four pairs of variables make up sixteen possible personality types (Figure 7).

The first letter in each group of four shows whether you are an extrovert (E) who is most at home in the outer world or an

Personality Types

ST	SF	NF	NT
ISTJ	ISFJ	INFJ	INTJ
ISTP	ISFP	INFP	INTP
ESTP	ESFP	ENFP	ENTP
ESTJ	ESFJ	ENFJ	ENTJ

E = Extroverted   I = Introverted
S = Sensing   N = Intuitive
T = Thinking   F = Feeling
J = Judging   P = Perceptive

Figure 7

introvert (I), at home in the inner world. The two middle letters in each group of four show how you receive data and how you organize it: whether you perceive the world by sensing (S) or by intuition (N); whether you make decisions objectively by thinking (T) or subjectively by feeling (F). The fourth letter indicates how you relate to the outer reality, whether you act in a planned or judging way (J) or in a spontaneous or perceptive way (P).

David Keirsey and Marilyn Bates have adapted Carl Jung's insights and Isabel Myer's method of measuring personality types in their book *Please Understand Me*. Keirsey and Bates discuss how various temperaments influence leadership style and effectiveness. They profile four kinds of leaders (they call them managers) whose style reflects the personality tendencies described above.

The *sensing-perceptive* (SP) leader is able to negotiate with ease and has a high sense of reality. He or she is often seen as a diplomat or troubleshooter, "good at putting out fires, at unsnarling messes, and at responding to crisis situations in a way which none of the others can match without great effort. Running through this style is a note of expediency—whatever needs to be done to solve the problem situation is done. Ties to the past and ties to the future are expendable."[7]

The *sensing-judging* (SJ) leader tends to focus on the organization as a body. He or she is an organization person, preserves the traditions of the organization, works for its stability, abides carefully by the established policies and operating procedures. "The SJ leader has a very special sense of social responsibility. He wants to know where his duty lies and then quickly get at it. The desire to keep busy with the discharge of his obligations is strong in the SJ. This sort of industriousness is also something he values in his subordinates, colleagues, and superiors. The hard worker is much admired by the SJ."[8]

The *intuitive-thinking* (NT) leader often is called the visionary leader and may find satisfaction in doing some kind of architectural or engineering job. NT leaders usually pride themselves on their intellectual capacities, especially when they have an opportunity to apply these capacities to the solving of complex problems. "He is not interested in maintenance or in consolidation, and he abhors unsnarling messes. It does not make much sense to him that crises should even exist, and to the Visionary things have to make sense. This leader can be adamant and stand on principles against all antagonists, no matter what the price."[9]

The *intuitive-feeling* (NF) leader is called the catalyst because of his or her personable qualities. NF leaders have the ability to bring out the best in people, possibly because they tend to focus not on the organization but on the individuals within the organization. "The NF is the natural democratic leader and the natural participative. His forte is a smooth, people-oriented process, with documents and product a fallout rather than a primary target. The Catalyst leader is comfortable working in a democratic climate, and is sympathetic to his people, generous with his willingness to listen to their troubles, and sincerely concerned with their personal problems."[10]

The Myers-Briggs is a standard testing device used by psychologists around the world. It helps us understand ourselves and other people, understanding valuable for effective leadership.

"Know thyself" was the counsel of the philosopher Plato. In the church we know ourselves to be children of God, created in God's

61

image, called to serve, love, and obey, and destined to abide in God's company.

To increase our leadership effectiveness it is helpful to know ourselves in more specific and intimate ways—to know the inclinations of our personalities and the characteristics of our style, to know the way others perceive and respond to us.

In addition to psychological testing and Clinical Pastoral Education programs, we can deepen our self-awareness through reading self-help books, using the Jo-Hari window, the Awareness Wheel, and the Myers-Briggs Type Indicator.

In the words of Edwin Friedman, quoted earlier, "The overall health and function of any organization depends primarily on one or two people at the top . . . and an organization tends to function best when its 'head' is well differentiated."[11]

5

KNOWING
YOUR
ORGANIZATION

Effective leaders know their organizations as well as themselves. They know their organization's "culture" as well as their own strengths, weaknesses, and goals. This general truth applies to organizations of all kinds, including the church. It also applies to the smaller groups that make up the church, whether leadership groups such as a church council or committee, a junior high class, or a women's organization. For effective leadership it is essential to know your group—its nature, its mission, its self-understanding—as well as how it functions.

The church is not easy to understand. One reason is that in the Scripture there are dozens of different images or metaphors for the church. It is family and flock; it is herald and institution; it is salt of the earth, light of the world, and new creation. Of the many images, however, the two most prominent are people of God and body of Christ.

The "people of God" image is a reminder of the human side of the church. We are "of God"—"called, gathered and enlightened" by the spirit, as Luther wrote in his explanation of the Third Article of the Creed; we believe Christ is present wherever two or three are gathered in his name. Despite this, however, we are people. Whatever else the church may be, it is always an organization of people.

But in addition to remembering that we are a people, it is important to remember that we are a unique people, a called-out people. As the second of the two most prominent biblical images for the church states, we are "the body of Christ." In the words of Paul to the church at Corinth, "Now you are the body of Christ and individually members of it" (1 Cor. 12:27). To the church at Ephesus Paul wrote, "We are to grow up in every way into him who is the head, into Christ, from whom the whole body, joined and knit together by every joint with which it is supplied, when each part is working properly, makes bodily growth and upbuilds itself in love" (Eph. 4:15–16). This image is a reminder that the church is always more than a human organization. As similar as the church may be to other organizations, it is still unique; it is Christ's body—owing its life and existence to the Spirit of God.

H. Richard Niebuhr maintains the necessary tension between the two images by talking about the church from two perspectives: theological and sociological. The first of these emphasizes the divine aspect of the church—the calling of God, faith in Christ, hope for the future. The other emphasizes the human side of the church—the people, the need of forgiveness, relationships with others, institutional forms. To Niebuhr the church is both human and divine, a dynamic theological and social reality.[1] For an adequate understanding of the church it is necessary to maintain the tension between the two.

The Lutheran confessions reflect both the human and divine aspects of the church, witnessing on the one hand to the church's divine source and reality and, on the other, to its human qualities. The following two statements serve as examples:

> The church is not merely an association of outward ties and rites like other civic governments. . . . It is mainly an association of faith and of the Holy Spirit in men's hearts.[2]

> We are not dreaming about some Platonic republic, as has been slanderously alleged, but we teach that this church actually exists,

made up of true believers and righteous men scattered throughout the world.[3]

The two dimensions of the church are also reflected in the Constitution of the Evangelical Lutheran Church in America. It states, on the one hand, that "the church is a people created by God in Christ, empowered by the Holy Spirit . . ." and, on the other, that it carries out its work through "congregations, ministries, organizations, institutions, and agencies," in other words, through human means.[4]

The church is both "people of God" and "body of Christ," both human and divine. While this paradox often results in tension over the church's goals, structure, and use of resources, it is a tension that cannot be avoided.

THE CHURCH AS PLATYPUS

Quite a different way of examining this subject is proposed by Philip Yancey in his article, "The Church as Platypus."[5] The platypus, writes Yancey, has a flat, rubbery bill and webbed feet like a duck, but a furry body and beaver-like tail. The combination of seemingly incompatible features gives Yancey hope that we humans can also break some of the rules that govern ourselves, especially such "organisms" as the church, which, Yancey observes, is also made up of contradictory parts.

Yancey compares the church to organizations and to organisms:

Organizations, such as the army, government, and big business, follow one set of rules. Organisms, such as living things, families, and closely knit small groups, follow another. The church falls somewhere between the two and attracts criticism from both sides. Organization people accuse it of poor management, sloppy personnel procedures, and general inefficiency. Organism people complain when the church begins to function as just another institution and thus lose its personal, "family" feel.[6]

Yancey acknowledges the inevitable tension between the two and then goes on to suggest ways of dealing with the tension in four different areas of congregational life: goals, status, structure, and failure.

Goals. Churches either make too much of goals or ignore them completely, says Yancey. While it is neither desirable or possible for a church to operate according to a strict management-by-objectives plan, the church ought not allow itself to be subjected to the whims and impulses of the pastor and a handful of others. The best way to operate, he says, is to see that some leadership people are relationship-oriented and others goal-oriented. This will help balance the organization-organism tension, and will possibly lead to the setting of goals where goals are possible while recognizing that important dimensions of the church's ministry are quite independent of measurable achievements.

Status. Yancey points out that in organizations, status depends on performance. When you prove yourself you get status. But in organisms status works quite differently. For example, how do you get status in a family? Something instinctively calls for fairness and equality, regardless of how deserving one may or may not be. In a church those with the status of position, such as pastor or choir director, should be encouraged to downplay the status factor by having sustained contact with people and groups of different status within the congregation.

Structure. Structurally there is often a sharp contrast between the way business and the church operate. Business usually has clear lines of authority and a carefully developed organizational chart. Churches usually do not. Why not? Yancey asks. "In the absence of a formal structure an informal structure will grow up. By defaulting on power, those leaders simply open the door to someone else's power. How many churches in America are held hostage by one power-greedy deacon or elder or a maverick music director?"[7] In the church, as in other organizations, it is appropriate to have a structure that will account for the varied abilities of its leaders.

Failure. Yancey reminds us that in the corporate world, people are laid off if performance consistently falls short of expectations. In organisms, however, things are usually handled differently. Families may have black sheep but they don't fire them. The prodigal son was welcomed back home; Peter was reinstated; even King David was restored to his place of leadership.

The Christian organization can hardly be that lenient, says Yancey, for ignoring an employee's failures produces at least three undesirable results. First, it tells other employees that there is no need to be conscientious about excellence or promptness. Second, the community at large concludes that you have no work standards and that therefore just about anybody can get a job with you. Third, the employee concludes that the work he or she is hired to do has very little value.

Yancey concludes: "Good management requires a balance between responsibility, authority, and accountability. Churches and Christian ministries must be accountable to a board concerned about efficient management and to the people funding the ministry."[8]

THE CHURCH AS A VOLUNTEER ORGANIZATION

While the church is both human and divine, and even something like a platypus, it also has many of the characteristics of a voluntary organization. Although, in the words of Luther's Small Catechism, we are "called, gathered, and enlightened"— and thereby hardly volunteers—we nevertheless belong to the church because we have chosen to do so. In American society, the church has many of the marks of a voluntary group.

Richard Hutcheson describes some of the characteristics of voluntary organizations:[9]

Authority. In voluntary organizations authority is in the hands of the members, not some outside person or group. Some of the authority is delegated to designated members of the organization who, in turn, exercise it in accord with the provisions set by the group as a whole.

Goal seeking. In voluntary organizations the goals are usually set by consensus of the members, the result of negotiation and joint effort.

Use of professional experts. In voluntary organizations the use of professional experts is limited to the number and type agreed upon by the members of the group. The professionals, however, are subject to the control of the members.

Compliance. In voluntary organizations compliance is voluntary, and is most often dependent upon the persuasiveness of the leaders and the goodwill of the members.

Organizational structure. In voluntary organizations the structure is usually democratic, providing for broad representation in decision making. Even when there may be a number of employed professionals, as in a large church, the control remains in the hands of the leaders elected by the group.

"To speak sociologically of the voluntary nature of the church may correspond to speaking theologically of free will in the faith response to God's grace," writes Hutcheson. "From the human perspective churches are indisputably voluntary in their composition."[10] And yet this must be kept in tension with certain theological perspectives, Hutcheson notes. In the church we believe God takes initiative. The church is under the lordship of Christ, and church members submit themselves to that lordship. The decision making of the church is done under the guidance of the Spirit. These convictions are all properly taken into consideration when we think of the church as a voluntary organization. Hutcheson concludes:

For reasons growing out of its transcendent dimension, then, as well as for pragmatic reasons, the church as organization must take seriously its voluntary nature. It is safeguarded against excesses of voluntarism—a "Gallup poll" decision-making—by the Lordship of Christ. And it is safeguarded against human autocracy in the name of the Lordship of Christ by its voluntary nature. Only by taking seriously processes derived from its transcendence, as well as processes derived from its human organizational character, can the balance be preserved.[11]

In its deepest being the church is a community of faith, dependent upon the call and presence of God's Spirit. Yet the church is also a human society that works through social and institutional structures. It is only through earthly entities that God becomes present and manifest. The church is both human and divine.

WHAT KIND OF STRUCTURE?

Whenever two or more people have dealings with each other an organization begins to take shape, a structure comes into being. The question is not whether or not to have structure. The question is, What kind of structure? To be more specific, given the complex nature of the church, what kind of structure should it have?

Peter Rudge identifies and describes five different organizational theories and interprets them in theological terms. He concludes that an approach in which the leader is concerned with both the organization's purpose and with its environment—which he calls the systems way of thinking—"has the greatest weight of biblical support and is nearest to the central stream of Christian thinking."[12]

But what are other possibilities? What is the role of the leader in each of them? And why does Rudge say the systems way of thinking is more in accord with biblical insights?

Five Organizational Theories

Traditional. The first of the alternate theories, the *traditional*, sees the organization as having a continuing life of its own. The phrase "maintaining a tradition" sums up the purpose of the organization, which usually has a long history and expects to continue into the future. The function of the leader is to help maintain the tradition. Teaching is important, for through teaching the next generation is brought up in the tradition. In accord with this view, the church leader gives attention to nurture and encouragement, providing for the spiritual sustenance of the people, conducting a priestly ministry.

Classical. The second view, the *classical*, sees the organization as having machinelike qualities—efficiency and rationality. The classical view is sometimes likened to a bureaucracy. Rules and procedures are laid out and the organization is operated from the top down. In this view the role of the church leader is largely that of an organizer and administrator concerned with the efficient operation of an organization.

Charismatic. The third view, the *charismatic*, is very different. There is little structure or organization. The charismatic approach involves cutting the roots of the past, overthrowing formalism, and launching out in new directions in new ways. Leaders here are not maintaining a tradition or running a machine, they are pursuing an intuition. They lead not by maintaining a tradition or by giving directives but by making personal appeals, prophetically and inspirationally.

Human Relations. In the fourth view, the *human relations view*, an organization is seen as a network of personal relationships within and between groups—the relationships often being informal, intimate, and fluid. Within a large organization there can be a multiplicity of groups, but because the focus is on the small group, there is little awareness of the other groups or the whole. The leader in the human relations view is seen as a small-group leader, providing at times democratic pastoral leadership. In the context of the church, according to Rudge, "The minister is envisaged as being in charge of an organization in which fundamental human rights are respected, leadership is exercised through persuasion, and response is sought through intelligent cooperation."[13]

Systems. The fifth view, *systems*, is most appropriate for the church, according to Rudge. He believes it has the greatest weight of biblical support and is nearest to the central stream of Christian thinking. In a system many participants act in an interdependent way so that the whole is greater than the sum of its parts. "The essence of systemic leadership," states Rudge, "is that the leader has a dual concern with the purpose of the organization and with its environment, both of which he interprets to the organization in such a way that the whole body may respond accordingly."[14] In theological terms, the "concern" would be the purpose and will of God for the world and the church; the leader's task is to clarify and express those concerns so that the church makes the necessary adaptations.

Rudge links the systems view to the "body of Christ" image of the church, seeing the various parts as members of the whole. St. Paul did as much when he described the church like this: "The body does not consist of one member but of many. . . . The eye cannot say to the hand, 'I have no need of you,' nor again the head to the feet, 'I have no need of you.' . . . If one member suffers, all suffer together; if one member is honored, all rejoice together" (1 Cor. 12:14, 21, 26).

I agree with Rudge and others[15] that the systems view is the most appropriate for the church. The traditional view tends to be too root-heavy for a changing world, narrow in its view of the church's purpose, confining in the way it sees the role of the leader. The classical view tends to focus on the organization itself rather than on its mission, and tends to treat persons as parts of the machine. The charismatic view tends to lead the church away from its biblical basis, depending too heavily on the vision or charisma of the leader. The human relations view neglects the wholeness of the church, the interdependency of the various groups and, as in the case of the charismatic approach, tends to neglect the "theological roots" of the church.

The systems view, however, is more flexible and open. It takes seriously both the biblical "givens" and the needs of the present, while honoring the wholeness of the church and the interrelatedness of its various ministries. It provides for an integrating approach to church life. As Alvin Lindgren and Norman Shawchuck state in their book, *Management for Your Church:*

If an organization is primarily task oriented, a bureaucratic style will prove most effective. If an organization is primarily person oriented, a human relations style will prove most effective. If, however, the organization understands persons to need organizations and structure in order to achieve its organizational goals, a systems approach will prove most effective, since systems theory holds the organizational goals and the goals of persons to be of equal importance. Systems theory addresses the interrelatedness and interdependency of the organization and its people.[16]

The systems view is a clue to understanding the structure and workings of a church and its various groups. As we see in later chapters, especially chapters 9-14, it is also the key to organizing such groups in adherence to biblical insights and for effective mission.

To effectively lead the church it is necessary to know the church, to know both rationally and intuitively its complex nature, its human side as well as its divine side, its two primary goals, its varied self-understanding. Knowing the church rationally and intuitively leads also to the appropriate use of power and authority, subjects we now consider.

6

KNOWING POWER AND AUTHORITY

Power both attracts and repels. While most people are attracted to a skillful and proper use of power, many are nevertheless ambivalent about it, often repelled by power as well as attracted to it. In the church, where service and self-giving are at the fore, it seems unbecoming to seek power. Power seeking may be another sign or expression of our sinfulness.

Shakespeare's *Macbeth* is the story of self-serving ambition for power. In the beginning of the story, set in eleventh-century Scotland, Macbeth is the model of a successful young nobleman—brave and courageous, yet gentle and patient for the throne. But when the king names another as his successor, barring Macbeth's way to the throne, ambition takes hold of him. Goaded by his wife, he one day sneaks into the king's bedchamber and stabs him to death. Because the heir apparent fears for his life, he flees and Macbeth is made king.

But Macbeth is consumed by guilt. He suffers terrible dreams, his mind is filled with remorse and distrust, his relationship with his wife deteriorates. Finally, when her growing madness results in death, Macbeth utters the famous line:

Life's but a walking shadow, a poor player,
That struts and frets his hour upon the stage,
And then is heard no more. It is a tale
Told by an idiot, full of sound and fury,
Signifying nothing.

(*Macbeth* V. v. 17)

Macbeth portrays the consequences of an unbridled quest for power, showing its moral and psychological effects. It confirms the truth of Lord Acton's statement that "power tends to corrupt, and absolute power corrupts absolutely."

We need not turn to the eleventh century to learn about the abuse of power. We see it in every century and in every society. James MacGregor Burns writes:

> Stalin controlled an apparatus that, year after year and in prison after prison, quietly put to death millions of persons, some of them old comrades and leading Bolsheviks, with hardly a ripple of protest from others. Between teatime and dinner Adolph Hitler could decide whether to release a holocaust of terror and death in an easterly or westerly direction, with stupendous impact on the fate of a continent and world. On smaller planes of horror, American soldiers have slaughtered women and children cowering in ditches; village tyrants hold serfs and slaves in thrall; revolutionary leaders disperse whole populations into the countryside, where they dig or die; the daughter of Nehru jails her political adversaries—and is jailed in turn.[1]

The church is by no means immune from the abuse of power. The excommunication of Martin Luther, the church's support of slavery in this country, the failure to send sufficient numbers of missionaries are examples of varying degrees of the misuse or abuse of power by the church.

The misuse of power is, in part, an expression of life in the world as it is, imperfect and incomplete. As Burns points out, "No organizations, of course, are free of power problems and conflicts. The question is how power, in a context of latent and overt conflict, is mobilized, organized, and managed—and to what ends."[2]

Power is not only a fact of life, it is a necessity of life. No power, no action. Before you can mow the lawn, coach a team, preach a sermon, there must be power. For the church to live and serve, it is essential that there be power—the power of people, ideas, and energy as well as the power of the Holy Spirit. Power may tend to corrupt, but the absence of power is inaction, and ultimately death and destruction.

Jesus was himself a person of power. While he exercised it in the manner of a servant, it is obvious from the record that he had significant power to forgive sins, heal broken bodies, clarify and proclaim the truth about God's Kingdom, and rally a community of followers.

The solution to the problem of power in the world and in the church is not to abandon power, erroneously concluding that we can carry on without it; nor is it to take the position that we can remain untainted if we keep our distance from power. The solution is to probe for deeper understandings of power, and then to learn how to use it as stewards of Christ and on behalf of his mission.

Psychologist David C. McClelland and consultant David H. Burnham identify three important leadership motives: the desire to affiliate, the desire to achieve, and the desire for power.[3] The first of these is essentially the desire to be liked by other people. The second is the need and desire to accomplish work projects or other challenges. But the third motive—power—is the primary motive for effective leadership. Wielding power, say McClelland and Burnham, is for most people more important than being liked or having a sense of accomplishment.

DISTINGUISHING POWER AND AUTHORITY

Max Weber's classic distinction of power and authority holds that power is coercive and that authority requires the consent of those over whom it is exercised. According to this, power is therefore inappropriate for use in voluntary organizations and churches, and authority is appropriate only when and if there is voluntary compliance.

Weber's understanding of the nature of power and authority seems to have little acceptance in today's world. While there are different views and understandings, authority is generally seen as the *right* to do something—such as the *right* to decide or to act—and power is generally seen as the *ability* to do something, or to prevent something from being done. These are the understandings we will use throughout this chapter.

Authority often goes with a position. A teacher under contract to teach at a particular place has the authority to conduct a class. A cook at a fast-food restaurant has the authority to prepare hamburgers. A pastor has the authority to administer the sacraments. A church council has the authority to hire a custodian. Each reflects the authority of position.

Sometimes authority seems to reside not in the position but in the person. When we say, "He carries a lot of weight," we mean there is something about his personality or experience that gives exceptional credence to what he says, that he has a lot of authority.

But this is more like power than authority, for power is the ability to get things done. "Authority," said John Gardner, "is legitimatized power, i.e., a mandate to exercise power in a certain sphere."[4] Unlike authority, power can be exerted anywhere; it is not confined to specific places or positions.

Psychotherapist Rollo May identifies and explains five different kinds of power.[5] A review of these is helpful as we seek both a deeper understanding of an elusive subject and insights for its appropriate use in the church.

Exploitative. This is the kind of power that gives the subject its bad name, identifying power with force. It is also a destructive kind of power, negative in its influence, harmful to those who experience it. Not surprisingly, exploitative power often leads to violence.

Manipulative. This is power *over* another person or group of people. Rollo May points out that sometimes manipulative power may be invited by the desperate situation of the person or group over which it is held. For example, years of economic hopelessness preceded the grasp of power by Adolf Hitler. At other times, however, power is imposed by strong but unscrupulous people who use it in manipulative ways, treating weaker people like pawns.

Competitive. This is power used *against* another. May emphasizes that competitive power can have both negative and positive results. Sometimes it puts the other into a losing situation. After all, if there is an opening for only one person to be hired, all who apply except that one lose out. On the other hand, competitive power can add zest and vitality to human relations. Some rivalry is stimulating and constructive. There is such a thing as healthy competition. To have someone against you is not necessarily entirely bad.

Nutrient. This is power *for* another. It is seen in the parent's care for his or her children, in the teacher's concern for the student, in the pastor's ministry to the church member. Rollo May says statesmanship at its best is also an expression of nutrient power at work. The president of the country is a father figure to many, one who has a paternalistic role and influence, expressing nutrient power.

Integrative. The fifth kind of power that May identifies is power *with* another person. Power that joins with the power of another resulting in greater power for both is integrative power. May said he thought of calling it cooperative power, but decided against that because sometimes people are coerced into cooperation. Integrative power, he says, is often the result of using Hegel's process of thesis, antithesis, and synthesis, with the ideas of the first person being critiqued by the thoughts of the second, leading to a new or possibly modified idea.

May cites the life of Martin Luther King Jr. as an example of integrative power at work. King said that his nonviolent approach "has a way of disarming the opponent. It exposes his moral defenses. It weakens his morale and at the same time it works on his conscience. He just doesn't know how to handle it."[6] This is integrative power, says May, because it depends for its effectiveness not only upon the courage of the nonviolent one but also upon the moral development and the awareness of the others.

Without the latter, the nonviolent approach would be ineffective, for it needs an appropriate response from the others.

May goes on in his analysis to say that the five different kinds of power are all present in the same person at some time or other. While nutrient and integrative power may be more honorable than the others, especially exploitative and manipulative power, May would say that none of us is immune from any of them. He concludes, "The goal for human development is to learn to use these different kinds of power in ways adequate to the given situation."[7]

The two kinds of power described last, the nutrient and the integrative, seem particularly appropriate for use in the church. "Nutrient" conveys the idea of nurture, one of the primary ministries and goals of the church. It is ministry *for* the other. Integrative power is compatible with the church's position on the "priesthood of all believers," as well as with the democratic or participative type of governance that is characteristic of most congregations. Nutrient and integrative power should be seen as the norm for church leaders.

TWO WAYS OF
EXERCISING POWER

With the help of Rollo May, we have identified five different kinds of power, and now with the help of James and Marguerite Craig, Robert Worley, James Burns, and others we examine different ways of exercising power.

The Craigs say there are essentially only two different qualities of power, two different ways of expressing it: directly or synergistically. See Figure 8.[8]

The "No Power" category at the bottom of the triangle is more imagined than actual, for all people have power to one degree or another. Nevertheless, some people feel powerless and most people lack the power they wish they had.

As the diagram suggests, power is usually expressed in direct or synergistic ways. The first of these represents the unattractive

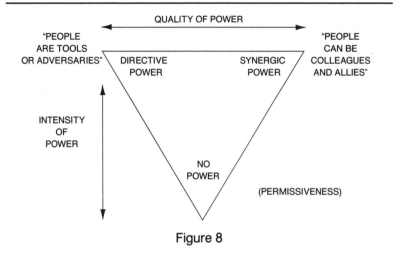

Figure 8

image of power, the coercive expressions, or what Rollo May called exploitative or manipulative power. It may be the expression of "naked power," of unreasonable and unnecessary force. In some instances such expressions of power are entirely inappropriate. If the church is on fire, someone should shout, "Everybody get out!" There are times when it is proper for one person to assume and exercise power in a direct way.

Usually, however, we prefer and advocate synergistic or shared power. This is especially true in voluntary organizations and churches. Robert Worley writes that the chief distinction between the voluntary and the nonvoluntary organization is the way power is diffused in one and centered in the other. In churches and voluntary organizations, the elected leaders have only a limited amount of power. They may have authority—the right to decide—but their ability to make things happen is limited because the power is so widely distributed. In Worley's words: "Power is lodged in every member and group. Each person has total control over his piece of power. Control of this power is exercised through attendance and contribution of resources (time, money, ideas, skills) to congregational goals. This is real power, as any budget and finance committee can attest at stewardship time."[9]

How can leaders gain more power in a church or voluntary organization? There is only one way, says Worley:

> Power that is made available to leaders must be developed through activating and mobilizing members. Power to achieve goals within the organization depends upon individuals and constituent groups contributing their power in such a way that leaders can use it. Persons are much more likely to share power, to contribute their resources, when the congregation incorporates their personal goals into congregational goals and then supports and encourages persons to work to attain these goals.[10]

Worley's insights are affirmed by an author with a quite different perspective, the historian and political scientist James Mac-Gregor Burns. Burns believes we have been too enthralled with power in our society, especially but not exclusively in the political realm. "Viewing politics *as* power has blinded us to the role of power *in* politics and hence to the role of leadership," writes Burns.[11] He then makes this remarkable statement:

> Our main hope for disenthralling ourselves from our overemphasis on power lies more in a theoretical, or at least conceptual, effort, than in an empirical one. It lies not only in recognizing that not all human transactions are necessarily coercive or exploitative. . . . It lies in seeing that the most powerful influences consist of deeply human relationships in which two or more persons engage one another. It lies in a more realistic, a more sophisticated understanding of power, and of the often far more consequential exercise of mutual persuasion, exchange, elevation, and transformation—in short, of leadership. . . . We must see power—and leadership—not as things but as relationships. We must analyze power in a context of human motives and physical constraints. If we can come to grips with these aspects of power, we can hope to comprehend the true nature of leadership—a venture far more intellectually daunting than the study of naked power.[12]

Without using the word, Burns goes on to describe synergistic power—not a property or possession but a "relationship in which two or more persons tap motivational bases in one another and bring varying resources to bear."[13]

James Maccoby apparently discovered expressions of synergistic or relationship power in his study of the lives and experiences of six leaders of varying backgrounds, one a foreman in an auto-parts factory and another a United States congressman.

> They don't try to control everyone. They involve subordinates in planning and evaluation of work, spending time in meetings so that the whole team shares an understanding of goals, values, priorities, and strategies. They spend more time up front developing consensus, but they spend less time reacting to mistakes and misunderstandings. They are skilled at leading meetings and turning off people who ramble or attempt to dominate.[14]

Women may have a greater inclination or gift for the synergistic expression of leadership. Anne Wilson Schaef implies this with her description of two different perspectives on reality: the White Male System and the Female System. The White Male System assumes there is only so much power to go around, Schaef observes. Consequently, the more of it you share with another the less you will have for yourself. In the Female System, however, "power is viewed in much the same way as love. It is limitless, and when it is shared it regenerates and expands. There is no need to hoard it because it only increases when it is given away."[15]

Schaef then examines briefly the different ways the two systems view the purpose of power. "In the White Male System, power is conceived of to exert domination and control over others. In the Female System, power is conceived of as personal power which has nothing to do with power or control over another."[16]

In accord with this, Roy M. Oswald and Joan B. Bowman of the Alban Institute in Washington, D.C., contend that the best leadership teams should have a man and a woman at the top, each complementing and strengthening the other. They state:

> There is more energy, compassion and vision in church systems where men and women share power in a synergistic fashion. In each

instance, that power, energy, compassion and vision will surpass the synergistic leadership of a same sex team. We believe priority should be given to developing model man/woman teams in key leadership roles in religious systems.[17]

Robert Terry, director of the Reflective Leadership Program at the Hubert H. Humphrey Institute of Public Affairs in Minneapolis, outlines the relationship of power to the other three main ingredients of organizational life: mission, structure, and resources.

Mission is the goal toward which action moves, structure is the channel of the action, and the resources are the basis of the action. Power is the energy that moves the action from the resources through the structure to the mission.[18]

Figure 9 is revised from the one provided by Terry:

Resources ———▶	Power ———▶	Structure ———▶	Mission
Things	Commitment	Planning	Meaning
Ideas	Passion	Process	Values
People	Will	Form	Vision
Time	Interest	Institution	Oughts
Space	Decision	Society	Hopes
Money	Dynamic	Group	Dreams
Commodities	Courage	Rules	Future

Figure 9

According to Figure 9, everything is drawn by the mission. You could also say that everything is shaped by the mission. In the words of Terry: "Whatever the goal, it is important to remember that mission directs power and that power energizes the push toward mission."[19]

CONCLUDING THOUGHTS ON POWER

At the outset we acknowledged with Lord Acton that power tends to corrupt. This will perhaps always be the case. Power seems to be addictive to many people, perhaps to all people. And just as there is a dark side to the human personality and soul, there is a dark side to the use of power.

But the potential for abuse is not reason enough to abandon power. In fact, as Burns said, power is ubiquitous—there is no escaping from it, even if we wanted to. To abandon power is to abandon life and responsibility. The key is to harness power for its proper use—to put checks and balances in place, possibly to separate power into two or more "branches" as does our federal government, and to tie the exercise of power to the mission of the organization, as in Robert Terry's view described above.

In the church, pastors obviously have a considerable amount of power. Ordination sets them apart and gives them authority to fulfill a role and perform tasks. They proclaim the word and administer the sacraments, signs of the power of God. Pastors are at the center of church activities and organizations, and thereby have access to information, providing them with the power that comes from knowledge. It is appropriate for pastors to have power. Without it they cannot fulfill their responsibilities, cannot serve in accord with their call.

But all members of the church have power. While authority may be in the hands of a comparatively small number, power is diffused and in the hands of all members. The task of leadership in the church is therefore the task of rallying the power of the whole, giving it what Rollo May calls nutrient and integrative expressions, and focusing it for effective ministry in the world.

The church is also concerned about the personal use of power—in marriage and family, in school and on the job. To stimulate thinking about the personal use of power, here are insights from theologian Richard Foster:

- In the individual, power is to be used to promote self-control, not self-indulgence.
- In the home, power is to be used to nurture confidence, not subservience.
- In the marriage, power is to be used to enhance communication, not isolation.

- In the church, power is to be used to inspire faith, not conformity.
- In the school, power is to be used to cultivate growth, not inferiority.
- On the job, power is to be used to facilitate competence, not promote feelings of inadequacy.[20]

Leadership is the exercise of power. Without power there can be no leadership. Understanding the dynamics of power enables us to use it in appropriate ways for the benefit of the church and its mission.

PART THREE

THE PEOPLE WHO LEAD

Leadership has an elusive, mysterious quality about it. It is easy to recognize, difficult to practice, and almost impossible to create in others on demand. Perhaps no other topic has created as much attention from observers, participants and philosophers—with so little agreement as to the basic facts.

David P. Campbell

Let the greatest among you become as the youngest, and the leader as one who serves.

Luke 22:26

As each has received a gift, employ it for one another, as good stewards of God's varied grace.

1 Peter 4:10

7

QUALITIES
OF CHURCH
LEADERS

What are the personal qualities of leaders? What qualities enhance their ability to lead? Albert Einstein mentions leadership qualities in a tribute to his friend and colleague, H. A. Lorentz: "His never-failing kindness and generosity and his sense of justice, coupled with a sure and intuitive understanding of people and human affairs, made him a leader in any sphere he entered. Everyone followed him gladly, for we felt he never set out to dominate but only to serve."

What Einstein refers to is not leadership skill or leadership style, but something less tangible, perhaps less teachable—qualities of the person that include attitude, perspective, and even philosophy of life. It is important for leaders and potential leaders to know what they are, and to nurture them in their own lives.

This seems to be the position of the Scripture on the subject. In the Bible leaders are of many different types and exhibit many different skills. But behind the various skills and types are identifiable leadership qualities.

From the writings of the apostle Paul we learn that leaders in the church are to be above reproach and of good reputation. Leaders are to be prudent and of sound mind, living well-ordered and respectable lives. They are to be gentle and hospitable. Covetousness and a love of money are to be shunned. Paul's statement to Timothy about overseers in the church sums up his position on the qualifications of church leaders in general: "An overseer, then, must be above reproach, the husband of one wife, temperate, prudent, respectable, hospitable, able to teach, not addicted to wine or pugnacious, but gentle, uncontentious, free from the love of money. He must be one who manages his own household well, keeping his children under control with all dignity . . . and not a new convert lest he become conceited. . . . And he must have a good reputation with those outside the church" (1 Tim. 3:2-7, NASV).

The apostle Peter's views on the subject are in accord with Paul's. He writes about the importance of being an example to others, about being properly motivated, fulfilling the responsibilities "not by constraint but willingly," and about having an attitude of humility. "So I exhort the elders among you, as a fellow elder and a witness of the sufferings of Christ as well as a partaker in the glory that is to be revealed. Tend the flock of God in your charge, not by restraint but willingly, not for shameful gain but eagerly, not as domineering over those in your charge but being examples to the flock. And when the chief shepherd is manifested you will obtain the unfading crown of glory. Likewise you that are younger be subject to the elders. Clothe yourselves, all of you, with humility toward one another, for 'God opposes the proud but gives grace to the humble'" (1 Pet. 5:1-5).

The emphasis of Peter and Paul is made against the backdrop of a more inclusive biblical emphasis: the concept of service. In the Old Testament the nation Israel existed as a servant to the nations. Even while trodden down by the military and political powers of the day, Israel provided a theology and morality that are the foundations of human existence and saw itself as a servant of God and of people.

Jesus took upon himself the servant role. He rejected the marks of status and privilege. He touched lepers, befriended children, washed the feet of his disciples, explaining his actions with these words: "You know that those who are supposed to rule over the

Gentiles lord it over them, and their great men exercise authority over them. But it shall not be so among you; but whoever would be great among you must be your servant, and whoever would be first among you must be slave of all. For the Son of man also came not to be served but to serve, and to give his life as a ransom for many" (Mark 10:42–45).

In his ministry Jesus assumed the roles of prophet and priest— speaking for God, as prophet, and, as priest, serving as mediator between God and people. Those roles undoubtedly shaped his servanthood, prompting him to give attention to the needs of people on the one hand and to the word and will of God on the other. But the most prominent image of Jesus in the New Testament is that of servant, through which he synthesized the roles of prophet and priest.

It is therefore no wonder that the New Testament has over 1300 references to servant, serve, and service. This perspective, prominent throughout the Scripture, is inherent to biblical religion. Servants cannot serve all of the wants of people, all of their desires and wishes, but they are concerned about the needs of people and of the world—whether they are spiritual, physical, emotional, intellectual, social, or cultural. Servants seek to identify the areas of need, and then take steps to heal, nourish, and strengthen.

Martin Luther said it well: "A Christian is the most free lord of all, and subject to none; a Christian is the most dutiful servant of all, and subject to everyone." The first part of the statement reminds us that we live by grace, not law, that in Christ we are free. But the second half of the statement reminds us that we are to use our freedom to be servants of all, not because we are compelled by the law but because we are moved by grace.

TRAITS THAT MATTER

In addition to the servant posture of the Scripture as a whole and the qualities highlighted by Peter and Paul, what else can be said about leadership traits and qualities? Again we turn to insights of social scientists, with the implication that they are adaptable for use in the church.

Warren Bennis and Burt Nanus, whose work was cited earlier, interviewed 90 effective and successful leaders—60 from business and 30 from the public sector. Their goal was to find the common traits in the 90 leaders. Amid all the diversity they discovered four common traits: commitment to a vision, effective communication skills, reliability, and self-awareness.[1]

By commitment to a vision Bennis and Nanus do not refer to a mystical or religious vision but to a frame of reference or an agenda that attracts and draws people and evokes their commitment. They point out that it is not the personality that attracts; it is the person's clear sense of direction, the focus of commitment, that has the power to enroll the other in the vision or cause.

The second trait, effective communication skills, is closely related to the first, for if others are to catch the vision, leaders must communicate what it is. Not all of the 90 leaders were good with words, the researchers found, but they were all able to communicate their vision in such a way that people were willing to affirm it for themselves.

The third trait, say Bennis and Nanus, is reliability or constancy. This does not mean that everyone else always agrees with the leader. It means rather that the leader's position is clear, and that it is consistent with the overall vision and plan.

The fourth and last trait uncovered by Bennis and Nanus is self-awareness. These leaders know their strengths and skills and deploy them effectively, discerning the fit between what they are good at doing and what an organization's needs are. One expression of this, say Bennis and Nanus, is positive self-regard, liking themselves well enough to nurture their own skills and competencies. A similar insight comes from the writings of Edwin H. Friedman, rabbi and family therapist. Friedman uses the expression "self-differentiation" to connote self-awareness, emphasizing its importance in all areas of life, in marriage and family as well as in leadership positions. Here is Friedman's basic concept of leadership through self-differentiation.

If a leader will take primary responsibility for his or her own position as "head" and work to define his or her own goals and self, while staying in touch with the rest of the organism, there is a more than reasonable chance that the body will follow. There may be initial resistance but if the leader can stay in touch with the resisters, the body will usually go along.[2]

The traits identified by Warren Bennis and Burt Nanus will serve effectively in the church as well as in business and the public sector. Church leaders, too, are committed to a vision and sense the need to clarify and communicate the vision to others. Church leaders, too, have reason to be reliable and constant in their lives and efforts, and to strive for self-awareness or, in the words of Friedman, for self-differentiation. An intentional practice of the leadership traits described by Bennis and Nanus can strengthen the effectiveness of church leaders in whatever capacity they may serve.

LEADERSHIP QUALITIES OF WOMEN

In our day we are beginning to recognize the special leadership abilities of women. While men and women are more alike than different, studies during the past decade or two point out that, whether by nature or nurture, women bring special qualities and traits to the leadership role.

James MacGregor Burns acknowledges that some people have been slow to recognize this because of the male bias reflected in the false conception of leadership as mere command or control. But Burns points out that leadership has a much broader scope than command or control, and he predicts that women will in time alter the style and role of all leaders. Burns writes: "As leadership comes properly to be seen as a process of leaders engaging and mobilizing the human needs and aspirations of followers, women will be more readily recognized as leaders and men will change their own leadership styles."[3]

What are the key differences between male and female leadership qualities? Edwin P. Hollander and Jan Yoder state that experiments "have found male performance tending to be exploitative and competitive, and female performance to be more accommodative and tension-reducing. In addition, both leaders and followers rated male leaders as being more concerned with task performance than were female leaders."[4]

Among the ten megatrends identified by John Naisbitt in his book by that title are three that call for skills in which women tend to excel.

- The movement to high tech calling for the need for high touch, "high tech–high touch";
- The movement from representative democracy to a more direct democracy;
- The movement from hierarchical frameworks to informal networks.[5]

Marilyn Loden, the author of Feminine Leadership —or How to Succeed in Business Without Being One of the Boys, also emphasizes the special leadership qualities of women. She asks, "Exactly what is the feminine leadership of which I speak?"[6] She answers:

I see feminine leadership as different from male-oriented management but equally effective. It favors cooperation over competition. Feminine leaders prefer to work in team structures where power and influence are shared more across the group, as opposed to a hierarchy where power is concentrated at the top.

The feminine style of leadership also tends to place strong emphasis on developing positive relationships with co-workers. [A] feminine [leader] tries to relate to employees in a more personal way than often is the case in the traditional male pattern leadership.

Feminine leaders rely heavily on intuition as well as rational thinking in solving problems. They focus more on long-term goals which are good for the entire organization, as opposed to short-term. And they generally prefer a "win-win" approach to conflict resolution instead of the traditional "win-lose" approach.[7]

Loden charts the masculine and feminine leadership models in Figure 10.[8]

Loden is quick to point out that the qualities of feminine leadership are not limited exclusively to women. The same traits are

QUALITIES	MASCULINE	FEMININE
Operating Style	Competitive	Cooperative
Organizational Structure	Hierarchy	Team
Basic Objective	Winning	Quality Output
Problem-solving Style	Rational	Intuitive/rational
Key Characteristics	High Control	Lower Control
	Strategic	Emphatic
	Unemotional	Collaborative
	Analytical	High Performance Standards

Figure 10

found in men, she maintains. And some women tend to exhibit more of the masculine traits than the feminine. "But the key distinction is that as a class, women exhibit these particular attributes to a far greater degree than do men. The fact that feminine leadership is a generalization, and may not apply to each individual, in no ways makes it less valid, relevant, or meaningful."[9]

CAN THE TWO BE BLENDED?

Alice Sargent, author of *The Androgynous Manager*, believes that the qualities of feminine and masculine leadership can be blended.[10] The appropriate style for our time, she says, is an androgynous blend of the masculine and feminine styles that combines the best of the male and female traits. She cautions against abandoning any successful traits a person already has. Men can learn from women to be more collaborative and intuitive, and yet remain results-oriented. Women need not give up their relationship-oriented style; they can continue to be nurturing

93

Instructions: Allocate points for the statements below according to how true each is for you. Turn to the end of the chapter for the key. Use the following scale:

Very True   7 6 5 4 3 2 1   **Seldom True**

____ 1. ambitious   ____ 9. competitive

____ 2. helpful   ____ 10. warm

____ 3. dominant   ____ 11. independent

____ 4. tender-hearted   ____ 12. soft-spoken

____ 5. analytical   ____ 13. argumentative

____ 6. loyal   ____ 14. yielding

____ 7. a leader   ____ 15. forceful

____ 8. affectionate   ____ 16. caring

Figure 11

while learning to be comfortable with power and control. John Naisbitt and Patricia Aburdene say, "We are reinventing the corporation into a place where intuition is respected and where the leader's role is that of a facilitator, a teacher, and a nurturer of human potential."[11]

Figure 11 is a short quiz that measures whether you are a masculine, a feminine, or an androgynous leader.[12]

Androgynous leaders are a blend of typical masculine and feminine characteristics. Androgynous leaders feel comfortable giving and seeking help; they experience a full range of emotions; they are both rational and intuitive; they are open and honest with themselves and with others. In today's world androgynous leaders may have a better chance of being effective than any other.

QUESTIONS TO ASK MYSELF

In chapter 3 reference was made to Janet Hagberg's book, *Real Power*. In her study Hagberg describes six stages of power, each of which is characterized by certain leadership traits or qualities.

Stage One:	Powerlessness. Low in self-esteem. Dependent.
Stage Two:	Power by Association. Still dependent but learning to be independent.
Stage Three:	Power by Symbols. Egocentric. Ambitious.
Stage Four:	Power by Reflection. Competent. Strong. Showing true leadership.
Stage Five:	Power by Purpose. Self-accepting. Calm. Visionary. Humble. Spiritual.
Stage Six:	Power by Gestalt. Comfortable with paradox. Ethical. Quiet in service. Wise.

Hagberg emphasizes that people can be leaders at any stage of personal power but they cannot be true leaders until they reach stage four—power by reflection. This is reserved for those who have experienced the "crisis of integrity."

> This does not mean to be totally perfect, but rather that we care and ask about the difference in right and wrong in dealing with people and organizations and take stands on issues that have been worked out inside. It means not lying, even if we may be served well as a result. It means saying what we genuinely feel and think. It means not always having our own way, but being able to compromise when appropriate. It means accepting our whole self and feeling all right about the parts that are not so sterling, accepting being human and imperfect, which may be what it really means to be complete. It means being worthy of trust and respect even from people who disagree with us.[13]

Hagberg goes on to point out that when you look for leaders for your organization you don't necessarily look at the people who already hold positions of leadership. You look, rather, for the qualities of leadership in people and then encourage them to become leaders. In addition to the descriptions of the stages and qualities of each, Hagberg lists a series of questions that she believes true leaders and potential leaders will tend to ask, questions that seem to be especially appropriate for church leaders.

- What are the ethical or moral issues raised by this problem?
- How will each party to this agreement be able to gain something long-term as a result?

- How could we encourage individuals in our area to operate at optimum levels of creativity?
- Why don't we commit ourselves to giving more and see what happens as a result?
- If we look at this from the point of view of what is the right thing to do, how would we approach it?
- What if we stress quality first, then quantity?
- If we redefine success to mean personal satisfaction or peace of mind (or something else), how would we motivate people differently?
- What if we trusted people to be trustworthy?
- What is our long-term vision in this area? How will it affect us?
- Intuitively, what do you think is the best approach?
- How could I be more helpful, useful to you?
- How can we keep people feeling renewed? What do we need to change?[14]

Church leaders are appropriately drawn to the higher stages of Hagberg's scheme, power by reflection, purpose, and Gestalt. They appropriately ask the kinds of questions on our list, reflecting on them in light of their particular responsibilities.

Church leaders are a servant people. We serve by leading, and we lead by serving. We do not always succeed, we are not always effective. Yet we have the exhortation of the Scripture, the model of our Lord, and the hope and vision he provides. Moreover, we have the research and the insights of those who have given the subject their special attention. The church's life and mission are influenced by the quality of leadership it receives.

Answers to the quiz. Add the points you allocated to the odd-numbered characteristics. Subtract the points you allocated to the even-numbered characteristics. If you have plus 16 or higher you are a masculine leader; if minus 16 or lower you are a feminine leader; if between plus 15 and minus 15 you are an androgynous leader.

8

PASTORS
ARE ALSO
LEADERS

It recently took a congregation in Minneapolis over a year to select a new pastor. The congregation was turned down by its first choice, which lengthened the process somewhat, but most of the time was spent interviewing and corresponding with various candidates, and discussing their suitability for the position. The call committee wanted the person who was right for their situation.

While not every congregation takes an entire year to select and call its pastor, this experience suggests the importance of the pastoral role in the eyes of the church. Congregations do not choose their pastors casually. They do so only after much deliberation.

This is because of the central role the pastor plays in the life of the congregation. It is the nature of the congregation's leadership that more than anything influences how a congregation will function. At the center of the leadership is one who can facilitate or block the enabling process in the congregation's life, namely, the pastor. For good or for ill, he or she is at the focal point of the life of the congregation.

Lyle Schaller affirms this view when he describes the role of the senior pastor as "number one medicine man, the tribal chief, and the chief administrative officer of the congregation."[1] As tribal chief the pastor sets the overall tone of the congregation and is recognized as its head. As medicine man, the pastor officiates at the sacred rites of the congregation—preaching, administering the sacraments, burying the dead, and visiting the sick. As chief administrative officer, the pastor either actually performs the functions of the position or takes responsibility for seeing that they are done. Whatever we may think of Schaller's titles, there is a ring of truth to what he says, namely, that the role of the pastor is central in the life of the congregation.

A CONFUSED PROFESSION?

As important as the pastor may be for the life of the church, it is apparent that there is uncertainty and role confusion among the clergy in this country. E. Mansell Pattison asks:

> Who is the pastor? And what is the pastor's role? Is the pastor an administrator, fund-raiser, preacher, prophet, teacher? Is the pastor a parent-surrogate for surly children, an unrequited-love object for lonely people, a holy stand-in for worldly people? Should the pastor be a symbolic model of virtue, an underpaid salve to people's conscience, a virtuoso demagogue of mustard seed faith, or simply the person next door who is doing his or her thing in community betterment?[2]

In a survey of recent literature on the subject, Richard Vangerud identifies ten different perspectives on the pastoral ministry.[3]

1. *The Pastor Director.* First proposed by H. Richard Niebuhr in 1956, this view accommodates the varied activities of life in today's church.
2. *The Person for Others with a Faith to Share.* This view emphasizes the personality of the pastor, seeing him or her as compassionate and understanding.
3. *The Seer, a Representative Leader in a Pluralistic Religious Culture.* In this perspective the pastor focuses on the ministries of Word and sacrament.

4. *The Symbol Bridging the Community and God.* This view rejects the professional or clinical model in favor of the role of the holy person.

5. *The Ecclesiastical Administrator Monitoring the Mission of the Church.* According to this view the role of the pastor is to see that the church fulfills its goal "to increase love of God and neighbor."

6. *The Sacramental Person Ministering to the Faith of the Community.* In this perspective ministry is ministry of Word and sacrament.

7. *Theologians of the Church in the Ministry of the Word.* This perspective emphasizes the theological dimensions of ministry.

8. *The Learned Theologian in the Church's Mission.* This view emphasizes the intellectual aspects of ministry, drawing from various resources in the service of the church.

9. *The Practicing Theologian Interacting with the Stuff of Ministry.* Here the pastor draws from the Christian tradition, personal experience, and the culture of the day.

10. *The Prophetic Statesperson in the Local Situation.* In this perspective the role of the pastor is that of a prophet—but functioning with the tact and wisdom of a statesperson.

The different views, writes Vangerud, "seek to come to terms with the demands of ministry in our complex, pluralistic society— the authority issues, the authenticity issues, and the multiple demands upon the minister's time."[4] The different views also reflect something of the uncertainty of the pastoral role in our day, as well as the varied needs and expectations of the church and its people.

The Alban Institute newsletter *Action Information* also cites ten different models of the ordained ministry and suggests that congregations and pastors use the list as a basis of discussion about pastoral roles and expectations.[5] The models cited are:

1. Counselor/Healer/Caretaker
2. Minister of the Word
3. Administrator/Manager of an Organization
4. Prophet/Social Activist

5. Social Exemplar
6. Ringleader
7. Community Personage
8. Celebrant
9. Spiritual Guide
10. Witness

The authors of the list of ten models do not propose one as being more biblical or appropriate than any of the others. They imply that all are valid, but that it is important for pastors and congregations to have a common view, or at least a common understanding of the various views.

That there are differing views is not a new phenomenon. In the 1950s H. Richard Niebuhr wrote about the uncertainty of the pastoral role. "Entering the ministry is more like entering the army," said Niebuhr, "where one never knows where he will land or what specific work he will be called upon to perform."[6] The problem, Niebuhr explained, is not the loss of Christian conviction or anxiety over professional status; the problem is "how to remain faithful servants of the church in the midst of cultural change and yet to change culturally so as to be true to the church's purpose in new situations."[7]

REASONS FOR THE PERPLEXITY

Niebuhr and others have cited the rapidly changing culture as a primary reason for the role-uncertainty and confusion of pastors. This has certainly been an important factor and will undoubtedly continue to be so in the future. I would argue for two additional reasons: an inadequate understanding of the church and the lack of an integrating role model for ministry.

In chapter 5 we considered the importance of knowing your organization, in this case the church. We cited different images of the church in the Scripture and highlighted the two that are most prominent—people of God and body of Christ. We also noted that the church can be viewed both theologically and sociologically, which honors both its human and divine dimensions. Another helpful way of thinking about the church is to note that it is both a community of believers on a pilgrimage of faith and an organization of people with much in common with other organizations of people. If the focus is on the church as the community of believers, the role of the pastor becomes that of a prophet, priest, or witness. But if the focus is on the church as an organization, the pastor becomes the administrator, guiding the body in its corporate life. Here, it seems, is the basis of at least some of the uncertainty and frustration over the pastoral role. For some pastors it may be the lack of awareness of the complexity of the church; for others it may be an unwillingness to accept the church for what it is: both a community and an organization. Whatever the case, the pastor who seeks to carry out his or her ministry from only one of the two perspectives will inevitably be frustrated, for a portion of the church's reality is being ignored.

The appropriate response is to accept and affirm the dual nature of the church and then to adopt a pastoral stance that is broad enough to include both aspects. Sometimes the pastor will view the church as the community of faith and, in turn, will serve as priest, prophet, caregiver, and colleague on the pilgrimage. At other times, the pastor must see the corporate side of the church and give its organizational life the pastoral attention it needs and deserves, functioning now as guide, director, administrator. Often the two must be held in tension, if not balance, for the church to remain strong and faithful to its calling.

AN INTEGRATING ROLE MODEL

The model I propose is one that provides for an inclusive perspective on the pastoral role, honoring the two dimensions of the church while integrating the many and varied functions of the pastor, thus reducing the role uncertainty experienced by many pastors while increasing their effectiveness and sense of satisfaction.

When H. Richard Niebuhr wrote about the "perplexed profession" in the 1950s, he went on to propose a role model called pastoral director. He saw this as a role that was "emerging out of contemporary study of the Bible, participation in the tradition of the church, the experiences and reflections of ministers in our day, and the needs of the time."[8] Unfortunately, Niebuhr never spelled out what he meant by pastoral director. In addition to the fact that "director" is a bit too strong for our emphasis on shared leadership responsibilities, this is perhaps why the image didn't catch on in the church. What I propose for an integrating role model is a revision of Niebuhr's model, called the pastoral leader (Figure 12).

Pastors exercise leadership in several areas of their ministry. In preaching, for example, pastors are obviously in a leadership role, even though the expression of it is different from what it is in the organizational life of the church. The same is true when administering the sacraments, presiding at worship, and giving pastoral care. The pastoral leader image may strengthen the way the pastor functions in each of these capacities, and it may provide the pastor with a greater awareness of integration and wholeness in his or her work. Although pastors do exercise leadership in these pastoral activities, it should be noted that they are usually carried out in the context of the church viewed and experienced as a community of faith. It should be noted, too, that the pastor always functions as a servant-leader—as a servant who leads and as a leader who serves.

The sixth of the functions, organizational leadership and administration, views the church as an organization and often calls for the greatest awareness of leadership responsibility and skill on the part of the pastor. The church as an organization of people is subject to the pitfalls of human organizations of all kinds, and needs the leadership and direction that human organizations need. The pastor is therefore not only the prophet, priest, and celebrant to the community of faith; the pastor is also guide, director, and leader of the church's corporate life. Those who resist this aspect of the pastoral responsibility need only remind themselves of who gets the blame when things do not go well in the congregation.

Lyle Schaller distinguishes between leaders and administrators. This is helpful since so many pastors tend to resist administration. Administrators tend to concentrate on the short-term concerns;

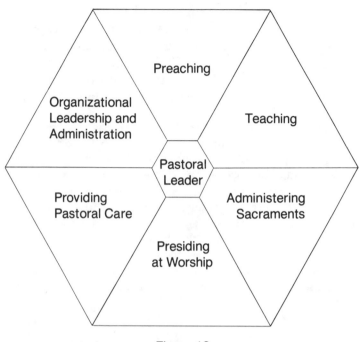

Figure 12

the routine, house-keeping questions; the issues of order and efficiency. Leaders focus more on purpose, mission, values, goals, and
roles. Writes Schaller:[9]

- The leader functions in a longer time frame.
- The leader understands and accepts responsibility for ask-
  ing the right questions.
- The leader has a clearly defined and determined commit-
  ment to reinforce specific values in the organization.
- The leader appreciates the distinctive contributions of elites.
- The leader understands the mission or reason for existence
  of that organization, designs the administrative structure to
  accomplish that mission, and is able and willing to turn that
  design into reality.
- The leader understands the value of allies and coalitions.
- The leader encourages rather than smothers creativity.

Leadership is more than awareness and understanding, however, more than perspective or attitude. Leadership is to be expressed in concrete ways in the life of the church. Of the 12 keys to an effective church, leadership is number five, says pastor and church consultant Kennon Callahan. "The time for leaders has come, the time for enablers is past," writes Callahan.[16] He continues:

> Leaders are those who effectively lead. There may have been a time when it was useful to think of them as enablers; certainly, the management philosophy that centered on the word "enabler" was a major contribution in overcoming the benevolent authoritarian styles of leadership of a number of pastors and key laypersons. To that extent the enabler movement has been useful. However, that movement has seen its day. . . . It is decisive that leaders lead the congregation forward toward the thoughtful accomplishment and achievement of substantive objectives. That means that leaders are active as well as responsive. That means that leaders share their own sense of direction and vision as well as simply enabling others to share theirs.[11]

THE PASTORAL LEADER
AT WORK

While pastors have leadership responsibilities in the life of the congregation as a whole, it is helpful to identify the particular areas of leadership and to note some of the differences between them.

Pastors serve as pastoral leaders with and for the congregation as a whole. As noted earlier in the chapter, when the pastor preaches, teaches, administers the sacraments, or presides at worship he or she is in a leadership role. The pastoral leader is a spiritual leader for the community of faith, holding before the community the vision and promises of God. He or she is encourager, appreciator, climatizer, a transforming leader who raises the levels of motivation and morality.

Pastors serve as pastoral leaders also with the staff of the church, whether the staff is a part-time custodian and part-time secretary or a staff of several pastors and lay professionals, and a variety of support staff people. Here the pastor (or in the case of a larger staff, the senior pastor) functions as head of staff, guiding and coordinating the work of the others. To be head of staff is not a position of honor; it is a way of working, a way of seeing that the gifts are directed to the needs of the church. This responsibility calls for knowledge and skills that are not normally gained through a typical seminary education. Workshops on supervision and personnel management and participation in some of the offerings described in chapter 4 can equip the pastoral leader for this aspect of his or her role.

The third area of leadership for the pastoral leader is with the elected lay leaders of the congregation. The best style is a shared leadership, sometimes called participative or consultative. We examined this in chapter 3, noting that the best style is not authoritarian or laissez-faire, but somewhere on a continuum between the two extremes, depending upon the particular circumstances.

When working with the elected leaders of the congregation, the pastoral leader will often take the initiative and make suggestions and recommendations. The pastoral leader will refrain from turning the elected leaders into a rubber-stamp group, but he or she will diagnose needs, provide information, and make proposals for the consideration of the governing board. In this way the pastoral leader empowers the elected leaders to fulfill their responsibilities. While some pastors tend not to make suggestions for the congregation's life and ministry, opting for the role of enabler instead of leader, recent research from the Alban Institute confirms what many would suspect, namely, that when the pastor sits back and waits for the laity to take the initiative, not much happens. The Alban Institute research indicated that in small congregations with Sunday attendance under 100, the laity tended to take the initiating role. But when Sunday attendance reached 200 the roles were reversed, and now the pastor was the initiating leader. And the larger the congregation grows beyond the 200 level, the clearer this picture becomes. The pastor is increasingly the initiating leader, whether or not he or she is comfortable in that role, and "any hope for a lay leader to influence the direction of a congregation rests in his or her ability to influence the pastor."[12] By taking the initiative, however, the pastoral leader can empower others and influence the entire congregation.

Myrna Christopher Kysar notes that pastors carry out a large portion of their ministry through program leadership, a fact that calls for leadership skills of various kinds. Among the responsibilities of program leaders, says Kysar, are these:

- The conception of program possibilities;
- Knowledge and assessment of program resources offered through the wider expressions of the church;
- The involvement of laypersons in the program;
- Oversight of the program. The pastor has the delicate task of gentle and wise supervision of those who have accepted responsibilities.[13]

Pastors are also leaders. Their effectiveness as pastors, as well as the effectiveness of the congregations they serve, is dependent to a great degree on how they assume the leadership role. I propose here a new model for pastors serving today's church, the pastoral leader—a model that integrates the various pastoral functions while freeing the pastor for leadership responsibilities in a church that is both community of faith and organization of people. Further chapters provide insights that help equip the pastoral leader for this role and ministry.

9

LAY LEADERS
IN THE CHURCH

The primary vocation and ministry of laypersons lies in their responsibilities and roles in society. The laity are to be the salt of the earth and light of the world, not the salt and light of the church. This is the deeper meaning of the priesthood of all believers and of Luther's concept of vocation. As Luther once said, the Christian cobbler serves God by making good shoes.

Yet some must do the many tasks in a congregation. Some must teach the classes, sing in the choirs, serve luncheons and receptions for funerals and weddings; some must usher and fold bulletins. Also—and here is the focus of this chapter—some must provide the necessary leadership for the congregation.

Much of what has been discussed in the previous chapters applies to the lay leaders of congregations as well as to pastors. Lay leaders, too, are called to be servant leaders, and are urged to see their service as ministry, not merely as volunteering at the church. Lay leaders, too, serve according to their gifts and in accord with their particular assignments. They, too, are to view the church as a body, a system, with many members or components, each of which affects the others. And they are to exhibit the qualities of self-awareness, of reliability, and of commitment.

A GOOD PLACE TO BEGIN

Having served as a pastor for more than 25 years, I have worked with dozens of lay leaders of various ages and qualifications. Some are eager to know what their authority is. They have had some concerns and when they feel they are in a position to make some changes, they want to bring the life of the congregation or at least one or two of its programs more in line with what they think it should be. The question is, What is my authority?

This is a poor way to begin, in part because it is a bad start in the eyes of others and in part because it is simply the wrong question. A better question is, What is my responsibility? And next, What is the responsibility of my committee? Two more are worth asking, How does my committee or group relate to others in the congregation? How can I best serve the welfare of the congregation? The authority question is secondary. First is the question of responsibility.

The service of "Installation of Elected Parish Officers" used in many churches gives a good summary of the responsibilities of lay leaders:

> You are to see that the words and deeds of this household of faith reflect him in whose name we gather.

> You are to work together with other members to see that the worship and work of Christ are done in this congregation, and that God's will is done in this community and in the whole world.

> You are to be diligent in your specific area of service, that the Lord who empowers you is glorified. You are to be examples of faith active in love, to help maintain the life and harmony of this congregation.[1]

THINGS TO KNOW

In addition to knowing its general responsibilities, the elected leadership of a congregation must know at least five other things in order to serve and lead effectively.

First, it is necessary for leaders to know the purpose or mission of the congregation as a whole. Some congregations refer to purpose and mission as being one and the same thing. Others see them separately, with the purpose as the continuing reason for being and the mission as the focus and emphasis at a particular time in the congregation's life. The congregation's constitution will state the purpose or, as the case may be, the mission of the congregation.

The model constitution for congregations of the Evangelical Lutheran Church in America, for example, has a statement of purpose that begins with a statement of identity: "The Church is a people created by God in Christ, empowered by the Holy Spirit, called and sent to bear witness to God's creative, redeeming, and sanctifying activity in the world." The statement of purpose goes on to list things that a congregation does: worship, proclaim the word and administer the sacraments, teach, serve, nurture, and manifest unity. The statement continues by referring to activities that are even more specific: provide pastoral care, witness, care for the sick and the suffering, and motivate the members to provide financial support. The very end of the statement of purpose in the model constitution says, "This congregation shall, from time to time, adopt a mission statement which will provide specific direction for its program."

Regardless of how a congregation describes its purpose or mission, it is important for the elected leaders to know what it is and to honor it as they carry out their responsibilities.

Second, it is necessary for the lay leaders to know the purpose or mission of the particular ministry in which they serve. If they serve in the ministry of education, for example, they will want to know what that ministry seeks to achieve. One congregation says, "To enable children to identify with and participate in the Church's faith, life and mission." Such a statement clarifies the purpose of the education ministry of the congregation and helps all concerned—teachers as well as committee members—to focus on the primary task.

Members of the congregational council, for example, will want to know the mission of the council. Again, the constitution of the congregation should have at least a summary of what those responsibilities are. Normally the council has general oversight of the congregation's life and activities, serving essentially as its board of directors. One council established for itself a set of goals that included the following:

- To review policies and goals for groups in the congregation to assure that they reflect the overall purpose and direction of the parish;
- To coordinate and link together all parish ministries and groups;
- To communicate the goals, policies, and decisions of the council to the congregation;
- To think about and discuss new ministries and new avenues for service;
- To see that the committees coordinate, develop, and evaluate the ministries and groups for which they are responsible;
- To work toward consensus in decision making and to encourage other groups in the congregation to do the same.

Fourth, the lay leaders of the congregation must know the responsibilities of the pastor, any associate pastors, and any salaried staff persons.

Pastors are normally issued a letter of call which spells out their specific duties and responsibilities. If a pastor is called to serve in company with one or more other pastors, either in a senior or associate relationship, then the responsibilities of each should be designated in writing. It is important for the lay leaders to know what the respective responsibilities are.

The official documents of the Evangelical Lutheran Church in America, for example, discuss the role of the pastor. In addition to such typical pastoral activities as preaching, teaching, and administering the sacraments, these documents refer to the pastor's leadership role which includes the supervision of the schools and organizations of the congregation.

Fifth, to serve effectively, lay leaders must know the relationship between the pastor, staff, and themselves as elected leaders. The question is, How can they form a leadership team that honors the gifts and responsibilities of the members and, at the same time, serves the welfare of the congregation and its mission?

While this subject is considered in greater detail in the next chapter, we highlight here some of its features.

In many organizations—business, educational, and voluntary—there is a careful distinction between the policy-making and the administrative or executive responsibilities of leadership. Our federal government, for example, separates the powers into three different branches: legislative, executive, and judicial. Most congregations would not want to operate that formally, but to think along such lines can help congregational leaders distinguish the different leadership responsibilities. The lay leadership of the congregation would then focus on the policy-making aspects of leadership—the legislative functions—and the pastor and staff would focus on the implementation of the plans and policies—the executive functions. While these cannot be kept strictly separate, nor would it necessarily be wise to confine the respective leaders to one or the other, it is helpful to make general distinctions and to say that the lay leaders generally concentrate on policy and pastors and staff generally concentrate on the implementation of the policies and programs.

In actual practice, however, the two may overlap. The pastors and staff influence the policy and plans of the congregation, bringing ideas and making suggestions and recommendations to committees and leadership groups, and the elected leaders often help with the implementation of the plans. When functioning in this capacity, however, the lay leaders carry out their activities under the guidance of the pastor or staff person. Senior minister Norman R. DePuy states this with clarity and emphasis:

> Regardless of how a church is organized, there are certain administrative principles that can help it involve a wide range of people and also avoid the pains that always result from poor administration. I would emphasize three principles, each related to the other, that can help us be better stewards of the time and talents we have for administration. First, policy and executive powers should be clearly separated, and, as a corollary to this principle, authority must be granted to match responsibility. The second principle is that committee appointments should be a means, not an end.

Finally, no matter the size of the staff or church, the senior minister should be the chief executive officer, reporting to the congregation through the council elected or appointed to represent the authority of the congregation.

The most important principle in church administration—as in any form of administration—is the clear separation of powers. The policy-making or legislative powers must be clearly and firmly separated from the executive or implementing powers. . . . Whether the staff consists of one or 15, the locus of executive power must reside in the staff, while the policy-making powers must reside in the appropriate committees or council.

The senior minister should be clearly seen as the chief executive officer, bound by policy decisions of the committees or council, but otherwise given the responsibility and authority to execute those policies.[2]

While the separate tasks of policy making and implementation may not always be as easy to distinguish as DePuy suggests, the basic position is sound, and when it is honored the result will be increased effectiveness and greater harmony.

For some, a better solution than the turf model, which says the committees and council are policy-making while pastors and staff do the implementing, is what could be called a continuum model. This model views policy making and implementation as closely related functions and allows the circumstances at hand to help determine the most appropriate roles and responsibilities for both parties. Some lay presidents and committee chairpersons have both the time and ability to implement programs while others have neither. A rigidly maintained turf approach prohibits responding with the flexibility provided by the continuum model (Figure 13).

While affirming the distinction between policy making and implementation, the continuum model acknowledges that the two functions are closely related and provides for a greater flexibility in the overall administration of the church. The elected leaders would still serve primarily in the policy-making role and the pastor and staff primarily in the implementation role. When pastors and staffs are involved in policy making they act in concert with the elected leaders; and when the elected leaders

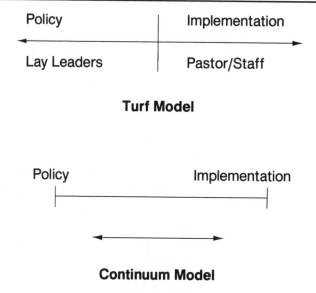

Turf Model

Continuum Model

Figure 13

are involved in implementation they act under the supervision of the pastor and staff.

THINGS TO DO

Having identified a number of things elected leaders need to know in order to be effective, we turn now to listing things for them to do. If you are a leader:

Be informed. Pay attention to what is going on in the life of your congregation and your denomination. Read your church's newsletter and your denomination's magazine. Be able to speak knowledgeably of your church's programs and its plans for the future.

Participate. Attend the meetings of your committee and be open to accepting a position of leadership in it. Active participation is a way to be informed, but it is also the best way to exert influence. And, of course, participate in the worship life of the congregation. Elected leaders should be in church every Sunday unless "providentially hindered."

Strive for consensus. There are times when consensus cannot be achieved, but at least strive for it. Split votes alienate people from each other. Avoid them whenever possible. To work for consensus, take time to discuss things in as much detail as necessary. Postpone the decision, if doing so will not have undesirable consequences. In general, plan ahead so there is adequate time for discussion before a decision is necessary.

Be goal-oriented in your work. Some committees and congregational councils are problem-oriented; others are activity-oriented. While committees will often deal with problems that arise and also with programs and activities, it is best to have a different orientation, namely, the goal or intended achievement of your committee and the ministry it oversees. This puts the other concerns in proper perspective. If you serve on the education committee and the goal is "to enable children to identify with and participate in the church's faith, life and mission," then that will give positive direction and shape to your committee work and activities, problems, and proposals will be viewed from that perspective.

Face outward as well as inward. Often lay leaders see themselves as representing the congregation in the policy-making groups. In a sense that is what they do—represent the people. But in another sense they represent the church to the people. Facing outward you become an advocate of programs and activities to the congregation. Members of the education committee, for example, will represent the congregation at large; but they also will be alert for ways to put in a good word for the education programs of the congregation. Facing outward, you can be an encourager in the life of the congregation, and in that way, too, fulfill a leadership responsibility.

While the primary vocation and ministry of laypersons is in and through their everyday responsibilities, some must do the tasks within the congregation and provide the services and leadership that its continuing life requires. Lay leaders, too, are servant-leaders, empowering and guiding the church's life and mission.

The next chapter provides further insights on how elected leaders can work with the pastor and staff on the congregation's leadership team.

10

THE LEADERSHIP TEAM

The cartoon in a magazine depicted a scene in a new and used bus lot. Pointing to one of the available buses, the salesperson explained to the prospective buyers that it was a special model for churches. "It comes equipped with two gas pedals, four steering wheels, and ten sets of brakes."

The subject of this chapter, team leadership, is discussed in different ways. Participatory leadership, consensus leadership, and consultative leadership are examples of terms used. People also speak of the empowerment of their colleagues and coworkers. Leaders are encouraged to see themselves as facilitators, not directors.

While John Naisbitt in *Megatrends* still finds hierarchies on every hand in the American workplace, he argues that our belief in their efficacy is on the wane.

What is evolving now is a network style of management. I am not suggesting that companies will become huge corporate networks, abandoning formal controls to allow employees to spend their time talking with each other. Instead, the new management style will be inspired by and based on networking. Its values will be rooted in informality and equality; its communication style will be lateral, diagonal, and bottom up; and its structure will be cross-disciplinary.[1]

In a later book, *Re-inventing the Corporation*, Naisbitt and coauthor Patricia Aburdene emphasize the same thing but state it more strongly:

> The top-down authoritarian management style is yielding to a networking style of management, where people learn from one another horizontally, where everyone is a resource for everyone else, and where each person gets support and assistance from many different directions.[2]

John Gardner also speaks of team leadership, while acknowledging that teams must still have a single leader:

> Most of the leadership that can be called effective involves a number of individuals acting in a team relationship. Teams have leaders, of course, and most ventures fare better if one person is in charge—but not as a solo performer, not as a giant surrounded by pygmies.[3]

In the church, too, we are learning about the value of team leadership. We speak of collegiality, of mutual ministry, of shared responsibility. While most church professionals were trained to be "lone rangers" in ministry, the emphasis on team leadership in our generation has prompted the church to reconsider some basic ideas, including insights from the Scripture, about team ministry. In the Scripture, interestingly enough, team ministry is often implied, if not forthrightly urged, in expressions of collegiality and mutual ministry. The concept of the church as the "body of Christ" led the apostle Paul to say in 1 Corinthians 12 that each member of the body is important to the well-being of the whole body. "The eye cannot say to the hand, 'I have no need of you,' nor again the head to the feet, 'I have no need of you.'" The clear implication is that the separate parts need each other, and that when all make their contribution, the whole body benefits. You cannot say, "I have no need of you," said Paul. "On the contrary, the parts of the body which seem to be weaker are indispensable, and those parts of the body which we think less honorable we invest with the greater honor . . . that there may be no discord in the body, but that members may have the same care for one another" (1 Cor. 12:22-25).

Paul's position is that every member of the team has a function, just as every member of the body has a function. Team ministry is clearly implied. Maybe the church is the world's secret leader of the principles and practices of what is now called "team leadership."

TEAM LEADERSHIP ON THE CHURCH STAFF

While much of what is said in this section applies to committees and other work groups, the focus here is on the salaried staff of churches, where there is at least one pastor and at least one lay professional or support staff person. In developing this section on the characteristics of well-functioning teams I use an outline from the Center for Parish Development,[4] amplifying it with insights from other resources.

A Sense of Common Goals

Members of a well-functioning staff are encouraged to share their expectations and concerns about the purpose and functions of the staff, developing a common goal for all to affirm. "The first essential of good staff relations is not a proper set of job descriptions or a definitive assignment of duties," writes Herman Sweet, "but is acceptance and understanding among the persons involved, and steadfast allegiance to a common overall purpose."[5]

A good example of a statement describing the purpose and goals of a church staff is the following, developed by the Lutheran Church of the Good Shepherd in Minneapolis:

The overall function of the church staff is to help the congregation fulfill its purpose: to affirm, interpret and express the Christian faith.

The staff works with the elected leaders of the congregation to determine policies and programs that will help achieve that end. The staff leads services of worship, preaches, teaches, guides, counsels, trains and initiates for the same general reason—to help the congregation fulfill its purpose of affirming, interpreting, and expressing the Christian faith.

The staff strives to be both Christ-centered and person-oriented in its work. This principle honors Christ as Lord and source of the church's mission and, at the same time, recognizes that the mission is to and with persons of dignity and worth.

Functioning as a team, with the senior pastor serving as director and coordinator, each staff member has assigned areas of responsibility and concentration. Together they work to help the congregation fulfill its purpose.[6]

Clear Role Expectations

On well-functioning teams the various members have a clear and mutually agreed-upon understanding of what is expected of themselves and each other. They understand how leadership will be expressed and how persons in authority, both themselves and others, will exercise that authority. The role expectations are expressed in position descriptions that are regularly reviewed.

Position descriptions can be written in different ways but they should include the following information:

- Title of the position;
- General description of the position;
- Primary responsibilities and duties;
- Accountability;
- Relationships;
  —to other staff persons;
  —to congregational committees.

Some position descriptions include compensation and benefits, but it is usually best to put such matters in a separate document. Let the position description describe the position; specify additional information in another way.

Attention to Interpersonal Interaction

All members are encouraged to participate, are listened to, and are welcome to express feelings. Well-functioning teams strike a balance between task accomplishment and relationships, and give time and energy to nurturing the relationships as well as to planning and coordinating the work of ministry. Douglas McGregor believes mutual support within the work group is essential for effective and satisfying team leadership. On the team, he states, there must be "caring, concern, help, friendliness and love."[7] If team members can be publicly supportive of each other, so much the better. And, of course, disagreements are resolved in private.

Encouragement of a Wide Diversity of Views

While a diversity of views can disrupt group harmony, such disruptions need not be permanent. Team members are encouraged to bring to the group a diversity of views—not, of course, to block progress but rather to enrich and strengthen the overall effort. Those who bring ideas and suggestions that are not seen to be immediately useful are encouraged to continue their creative thinking.

Positive Use of Power

On well-functioning teams, the influence and power of members is openly recognized and is used to foster group goal setting and decision making, and also to support others in fulfilling their responsibilities. Persons with power seek to empower others, rather than dominate discussions and decisions or impose their individual goals upon the group.

In his research for *Peak Performers,* Charles Garfield found that a characteristic of many high achievers is the ability to empower others. This does not mean "giving away your strength" to someone else as did Samson to the Philistines. On the contrary, peak performers discover time and again that releasing the power in others, whether in coworkers or customers, benefits them in the long run; the more they empower, the more they achieve, and the more successful the whole enterprise becomes."[8] Nutrient and integrative power, considered in chapter 6, are seen as the most appropriate expressions of power.

Open Communication

Well-functioning teams experience open communication between the members and within the team. Open communication, which can be described as assertive communication in which team members take responsibility for getting their own messages across and also for hearing what others are saying, contributes much to the operation of the team. Through communication team members make known their thoughts, hopes, desires, questions, knowledge, and plans. Through communication team members inform, persuade, consult, recognize, appreciate, and participate.

Good communication usually doesn't happen without encouragement and without provision for time and place. One way to foster good communication is to hold regular meetings of the staff, at least weekly, at which time there is opportunity for worship and fellowship, as well as for planning and scheduling. Another way is to hold annual or semiannual retreats, away from the daily round, for deeper discussion of some of the work issues, as well as for activities and discussions that strengthen communication and relationships.

Open Dealing with Conflict

Conflicts are accepted as normal by a well-functioning team, and members are encouraged to see them as providing opportunity for growth and learning. Individuals may serve as third-party consultants when members of the team are in conflict with one another, helping to identify the problem, the differences, and the overlap of concerns that can be explored together. It may be wise to have a formal procedure for handling staff conflict. One congregation stated theirs as follows:

Staff members are to discuss any staff differences or work dissatisfactions first with the pastor. If the problem is not satisfactorily resolved, the staff member may then consult with the president of the congregation.

The president of the congregation, while maintaining open communication with the pastor, will seek to mediate the differences and/ or dissatisfactions, and at his or her own discretion of or upon the request of the staff member involved shall provide for a meeting with the Personnel Committee.

Staff members shall present their differences and/or work dissatisfactions to the Personnel Committee in writing. This will not become a part of the congregation's permanent records, but will be destroyed when the issue is resolved.[9]

As stated, this is a formal procedure that may be used infrequently. Whenever possible it is best to deal with conflict in a less formal way, using the existing relationships of trust and responsibility. For additional information on the management of conflict, see chapter 13.

Adequate Decision-Making Procedures

In well-functioning teams the members are skilled at diagnosing a situation and at taking steps to reach the necessary decision. Members of the team will know the limits of their own decision-making authority, as will the team as a whole, and will know the next step in the process. Is it the pastor? The chairperson? The board? Sometimes the team will have to decide upon the next step.

The above characteristics of well functioning teams can serve as a checklist for leadership teams of various kinds, helping teams assess their operating effectiveness, discover clues as to where problems may lie, and build a stronger, more productive team while providing deeper satisfaction for the members.

In addition, we identify and discuss three other matters of importance for the church's leadership team.

SELECTION OF THE STAFF

For an effective team ministry it is desirable—even necessary—to have a variety of gifts and talents on the church staff. While there is a point at which diversity becomes incompatibility, resulting in insufficient consensus and ineffectiveness, a diversity of gifts is nevertheless desirable.

Here are three considerations for staff selection: competence, compatibility, and commitment.

Competence is the ability to do what needs to be done, knowing the job and doing it well. Whether the position is that of pastor, education director, organist, or custodian, competence is called for. People grow in competence through experience and continuing education, but a significant level is required at the beginning. Before calling or employing ask, What is this person's track record? What competencies has he or she exhibited in the past? Accurate answers to the questions are essential.

Compatibility has two essential ingredients: a similar theology and view of the church, and a work ethic that complements the others on the team. If the members of the team do not have a similar theological outlook, they will eventually be working at cross-purposes. If the team members do not have a similar work ethic, there will be continuing friction and disappointment with one another on the team. In selecting members for the team, be alert to compatibility.

Take seriously, too, commitment—commitment to God, to the life and ministry of the church, and to the particular church that he or she will be serving. Church staff members earn their living by working in and serving the church; but shy away from anyone who seems to be primarily earning a living—who is looking for a job "because I've got to make a living." Their commitment may leave much to be desired.

Who should select the members of the staff? Most congregations stipulate that the congregation as a whole calls its pastors, usually upon the recommendation of a call committee. The documents of congregations normally provide for the means of selecting other members of the staff, and are normally employed by the congregational council. The pastor (or when there is more than one, the senior pastor) should always be involved in the selection of staff. The final selection must be mutually agreeable to pastor and committee.

PROVISION FOR AUTHORITY, RESPONSIBILITY, AND ACCOUNTABILITY

In his study entitled *Psychological and Theological Relationships in the Multiple Staff Ministry*, Kenneth R. Mitchell discusses several principles of staff functioning, many of which affirm what is outlined above. An additional principle, however, has to do with authority, responsibility, and accountability. Mitchell writes:

It is important that each member of the staff have clearly defined functions and tasks for which he is: (a) provided with sufficient authority to insure performance of the functions; (b) responsible to the staff, the governing bodies of the church, and the congregation; and (c) accountable to the senior pastor or some other person with the authority of supervision or review.[10]

To be responsible, according to Mitchell, is to be in a situation in which you see yourself as called upon to respond to a wide variety of possibilities and needs. For example, a responsible person would pay simultaneous attention to the standards of the profession, to the needs of the church, to his or her inner integrity and relationship to God. Accountability, however, is another matter, says Mitchell.

It has to do with a clearly defined requirement that an account or description of one's activities is owed to a particular person. Accountability thus provides for the appraisal of the use of both authority and responsibility. . . . Authority, then, relates the minister to the task and to the tools by which he performs the task; responsibility relates him to the situation and the principle to which he is to respond; accountability relates him to a person or persons with an appraising or teaching or supervisory function.[11]

The accountability of team members to the team leader may be fulfilled in three particular ways—by sharing work plans, including the proposals he or she intends to make to the responsible committee; by keeping the leader informed of the progress of the various programs and projects; and by informing the leader of any serious problems that will prohibit the timely fulfillment of the plans. Accountability is fulfilled by sharing plans, progress, and problems.

PROVISION FOR PERFORMANCE REVIEWS

While the idea of performance reviews in the church raises both eyebrows and questions—How can you evaluate the Holy

Spirit?—it is helpful nevertheless to receive and give comments about how one's work and ministry seem to be progressing. For example, the team leader can reflect with a staff member on his or her competence level, pointing out areas of strength and areas where growth is called for. The same can be said about the person's work ethic. Is the person dependable, loyal, and punctual? How are his or her relationships with other members of the staff and with the congregation?

If it is understood that the intent is to affirm and strengthen the other's work and ministry, and if it is understood that the team leader has the right and responsibility to conduct the review, the whole process can be beneficial to the individual, to the team, and to the congregation.

STAFF COVENANT

To help assure that communication is kept open and that there is opportunity for two-way conversation on a variety of important matters, members of a team might consider entering into covenant with one another. As an example, here is a pastoral covenant developed by the two pastors of one congregation:

For the welfare of the congregation and its ministry, and in order to facilitate their individual and collective ministries, the pastors of _____ make the following covenant.

1. We will view ourselves as trusted supporters of each other, professional colleagues in the work of ministry, giving due regard to the role and responsibilities of the other.

2. We will carry out our work in close collaboration with each other, consulting and communicating regularly and openly, sharing both the joys and stresses of our ministries.

3. We will refrain from criticizing the other in the presence of members of the congregation and staff, and will seek to put the best construction on what the other does.

4. We will refrain from commiserating with persons who complain about the other. Instead we will seek to resolve any such complaints. If we are unable to do so, we will encourage the

person(s) to go to the other with the complaint. In either case, we will share the information with the other.

5. If one of us consents to being interviewed by another congregation or calling agency, the other will be informed prior to the interview and given opportunity to respond.

6. At least twice each year we will tell the other what we like about the existing work relationship and what we wish could be changed.

7. At least once each year we will discuss with each other our commitments outside the congregation and how they are affecting our work and relationship.

8. At least once each year we will review this covenant, changing and renewing it as we mutually agree.

A book that further describes the development of covenants and other aspects of working together as a staff is *Improving Your Multiple Staff Ministry* by Anne Marie Nuechterlein (Minneapolis: Augsburg, 1989).

STAFF AND ELECTED LEADERS IN TEAM MINISTRY

In an earlier chapter we considered the church as a system, or, in theological language, as a body with many parts, each one influencing the other and together influencing the whole. This model of the church emphasizes the interdependency of the various aspects of the church and also its capacity to meet changing needs. In evaluating this model of the church, James C. Fenhagen states that its strength is "that it places heavy emphasis on shared authority and mutual ministry, encouraging persons to move from a posture of dependence to that of broad interdependence."[12]

The systems view of the church enables us to view the church as a living system, even as an organism, as St. Paul does in viewing the church as a body. It means that groups and committees in the church are not autonomous, isolated, and independent of the others. Rather, they are joined together as members of a body, with each part interrelated.

Among the implications is that church staffs and governing committees are also leadership teams, and are part of an overall, integrating team, the congregational council. Here is one way to coordinate the many facets of church governance:

First, recognize the different leadership groups—the staff that was discussed in the first part of this chapter; the program committees that give attention to the various activities of the congregation, each of which has a chairperson; the congregational council which is given the authority to govern the affairs of the congregation.

Second, clarify the overall and unifying purpose of the various leadership groups, for example: to enable the congregation to fulfill its mission of affirming, interpreting, and expressing the Christian faith.

Third, establish the general responsibilities of each leadership group. The committees and council serve primarily, but not exclusively, in a legislative or policy-making capacity; the staff serves primarily, but not exclusively, in an executive or administrative capacity, having the responsibility of leading the implementation of the congregation's ministries and programs.

Fourth, establish a procedure that will honor all responsibilities and at the same time provide for broad participation. Here is an example of such a procedure:

- Staff members and committee chairpersons consult regarding the agenda for the next meeting.
- Staff members meet in an agenda-sharing session, to inform, to invite input, to coordinate.
- Pastors and council executive committee review minutes of program committee meetings and establish the agenda for the council meeting.
- At the council meeting, each committee chairperson brings a report and any recommendations for action.
- Pastors give pastoral reports to inform on various aspects of congregational life; sometimes to request action or invite counsel.
- Decisions of the committees and council are implemented under the direction of the appropriate staff person(s).

Fifth, each spring and early summer the staff and committees develop plans for the upcoming year. The overall integrated plan is approved by the congregational council, after which copies are made available to the members of the congregation as a whole.

IS YOUR GROUP IN NEED OF TEAM BUILDING?

Here is a checklist that will help determine if your staff, committee, or work group is in need of team building.[13] It measures the possible need for goal and role clarification.

Instructions: Evaluate your group by circling the appropriate number.

	Low Evidence		Some Evidence		High Evidence
1. Gripes and complaints.	1	2	3	4	5
2. Confusion about responsibilities.	1	2	3	4	5
3. Unclear goals.	1	2	3	4	5
4. Incomplete or inaccurate.	1	2	3	4	5
5. Arguments or bickering.	1	2	3	4	5
6. Communication breakdowns.	1	2	3	4	5
7. People feeling that they have to do the work of others.	1	2	3	4	5
8. People blaming others for problems.	1	2	3	4	5
9. Some work goes undone.	1	2	3	4	5
10. Low commitment to goals.	1	2	3	4	5
11. People failing to put forth any extra effort.	1	2	3	4	5
12. Confusion about when to help each other.	1	2	3	4	5

The church may be the world's secret leader of the principles and practices of team leadership, as we said. The diversity within the church enriches its life. The person and Spirit of Christ, together with his commission to the church, provide unity and coherence for the leadership team and for the congregation as a whole.

Interpretation of the checklist. Total the points that you circled. If below 20 there is little evidence of the need for team building. If 21 to 39 there is some evidence that your group would benefit from team building. Above 40 is strong evidence of such need.

PART FOUR

KEY
LEADERSHIP
TASKS

Pastoring in the twentieth century requires two things: one, to be a pastor, and two, to run a church. They aren't the same thing.

Eugene H. Peterson

Leadership is delivered through actions, through planning and implementing, through cajoling and rewarding, through persuasion and compromise, through detailing and demanding and driving ahead.

David C. Campbell

11

VISIONING
AND
PLANNING

The Christopher Columbus Award is given in jest to the person who is responsible for fouling up a project or plan. It is explained like this: When Columbus set out to discover the new world, he didn't know where he was going. When he got to America he didn't know where he was. And when he returned home he didn't know where he had been.

This chapter is written to help pastors and other leaders avoid getting the Christopher Columbus Award.

"WHERE THERE IS NO VISION
THE PEOPLE PERISH"

The statement from Proverbs 29:18 is a reminder of the significance of a future orientation, of plans, expectations, and hope. A vision gives life. And if there is no vision, the seeds of death are being sown and it is just a matter of time until death will prevail. Robert Greenleaf writes about this, using "dream" for "vision."

Not much happens without a dream. And for something great to happen, there must be a great dream. Behind every great achievement is a dreamer with great dreams. Much more than a dreamer is required to bring it to reality; but the dream must be there first.[1]

When Warren Bennis and Burt Nanus studied the work patterns of 90 prominent leaders, they discovered that one of the common denominators was a sense of vision. "All ninety people interviewed had an agenda, an unparalleled concern with outcome. Leaders are the most results-oriented individuals in the world, and results get attention. . . . Their visions or intentions are compelling and pull people toward them. Intensity coupled with commitment is magnetic. Vision grabs."[2]

Bennis and Nanus then state why a vision is essential to leadership success.

When the organization has a clear sense of its purpose, direction, and desired future state and when this image is widely shared, individuals are able to find their roles both in the organization and in the larger society of which they are a part. This empowers individuals and confers status upon them because they can see themselves as part of a worthwhile enterprise. They gain a sense of importance, as they are transformed from robots blindly following instructions to human beings engaged in a creative and purposeful venture. When individuals feel that they can make a difference and that they can improve the society in which they are living through their participation in an organization, then it is much more likely that they will bring vigor and enthusiasm to their tasks and that the results of their work will be mutually reinforcing. Under these conditions, the human energies of the organization are aligned toward a common end, and a major precondition for success has been satisfied.[3]

Charles Garfield discovered the same thing when he studied those whom he called "peak performers." Vision is what counts. Peak performers organize their actions around intended results, says Garfield. They affirm and communicate a clear mission, and they follow with a plan of action that includes specific goals, complete with benchmarks for measuring progress and results.[4]

Tom Peters and Nancy Austin agree. The techniques of leadership are not enough, they say in *A Passion for Excellence*.

> You have to know where you're going, to be able to state it clearly and concisely—and you have to care about it passionately. That all adds up to vision, the concise statement/picture of where the company and its people are heading, and why they should be proud of it.[5]

The quotation from Proverbs, "Where there is no vision the people perish," had to do with the well-being and effectiveness of a people called to be a blessing to the nations of the world. The same promise (and warning!) applies to the church in our time, and to every congregation, however large or small. If there is no vision—no dream, plan, or captivating intention—the congregation will be in the doldrums; they will not be the vital people that the Spirit calls them to be. On the other hand, if the congregation has a clear sense of mission and a vision for the future, you can expect the people to exhibit courage and vitality. This is confirmed by the research of Daniel V. Biles III, who interviewed pastors and lay people from nearly 40 churches in seven different states. Biles looked for the signs of excellence in parish life and ministry and repeatedly discovered a sense of mission.

> Having a clear and commonly held understanding of what ministry is and how it is to be carried out in a given parish. Strong congregations, to adapt the words of Tevye, the milkman in *Fiddler on the Roof*, know who they are and what God expects them to do. More than this, they do it.[6]

FINDING THE DREAM

How do we bring the vision into focus? How do we find the dream? One thing is sure, say Peters and Austin: "Visions cannot be concocted!" Nor is there any set formula, except that "it must come from the market and the soul simultaneously."[7]

From their research Bennis and Nanus concluded that most leaders are synthesizers of ideas from others and that the vision of their enterprise is actually a composite. While historians tend to write about leaders as if they created their vision out of some mysterious inner resource, in most cases the development is much more mundane. As Bennis and Nanus point out, John Kennedy spent a lot of time reading history, Martin Luther King Jr. studied the ethical and religious insights of his own and other traditions, and Lenin was influenced by the writings of Karl Marx. In each of these cases, the well-known leader may have chosen the idea or image and gave it form and clear expression, but most likely did not conceive of the vision in the first place.

> Therefore, the leader must be a superb listener, particularly to those advocating new or different images of the emerging reality. . . . Most leaders also spend a substantial portion of their time interacting with advisers, consultants, other leaders, scholars, planners, and a wide variety of other people both inside and outside their own organizations in this search. Successful leaders, we have found, are great askers, and they do pay attention.[8]

Not only did Bennis and Nanus find leaders to be listeners and learners, they found them to be great synthesizers, "masters at selecting, synthesizing, and articulating an appropriate vision of the future."

> If there is a spark of genius in the leadership function at all, it must lie in this transcending ability, a kind of magic, to assemble—out of all the variety of images, signals, forecasts and alternatives—a clearly articulated vision of the future that is at once simple, easily understood, clearly desirable, and energizing.[9]

Who does the church leader ask? Who does he or she listen to? Where does the church leader turn to get the "variety of images, signals, forecasts, and alternatives" needed to find or develop a dream for the church?

Consider four sources: Scripture, the congregation, the community, and the world.

Scripture

Because we view Scripture as the "authoritative source and norm of our faith and life," we appropriately turn to it as our primary resource for the vision of the church.

Scripture reveals, for one thing, that God has a vision for the world, that God can be called the great master planner who had a vision for all human history even before the earth existed. As St. Paul wrote to the Ephesians:

> Blessed be the God and Father of our Lord Jesus Christ, who has blessed us in Christ with every spiritual blessing in the heavenly places, even as he chose us in him before the foundation of the world, that we should be holy and blameless before him. He destined us in love to be his sons through Jesus Christ, according to the purpose of his will, to the praise of his glorious grace which he freely bestowed upon us in the beloved. In him we have redemption through his blood, the forgiveness of our trespasses, according to the riches of his grace which he lavished upon us. For he has made known to us in all wisdom and insight the mystery of his will, according to his purpose which he set forth in Christ as a plan for the fulness of time, to unite all things, things in heaven and things on earth.
>
> (Eph. 1:3–10)

According to the apostle, we were destined to be God's children before the foundation of the world. Moreover, God's plan and intent is to overcome the divisions of the world and to unite all things in Christ. Paul says that God is pro-active and intentional.

In Scripture God's purpose is described in different ways. God "desires all men to be saved and come to the knowledge of the truth" (Tim. 2:4). "God was in Christ reconciling the world to himself, not counting their trespasses against them, and entrusting to us the message of reconciliation" (2 Cor. 6:19). "For God so loved the world that he gave his only Son, that whoever believes in him should not perish but have eternal life" (John 3:16).

From Scripture we learn that God's purpose is redemptive, that instead of merely blessing the status quo, God is out to change it, restoring it to God's intention. In Scripture God is a purposeful God, with the final vision being that of a new heaven and new earth.

From Scripture we learn that the church is a called and commissioned people, existing for the welfare of the world and in accord with God's purpose for the world. The church is God's commissioned people, Christ's redemptive body, seeking always to be the salt of the earth and the light of the world.

The church is oriented toward the future. As Jurgen Moltmann has written, eschatology is not a loosely attached appendix to Christian thought; it is rather the basis of Christian hope, resulting in a people who are "forward looking and forward moving, and therefore revolutionizing and transforming the present."[10]

Moltmann goes on to link his theology of hope to the subject of planning in the church, an important way of giving expression to the vision. "Unless hope has been aroused and is alive, there can be no stimulation for planning. Without specific goals toward which hope is directed, there can be no decision about the possibilities of planning. . . . Planning must be aware of its origin in hope and the projection of hope. If it puts itself in the place of hope, it loses the transcendent impetus of hope and finally also loses itself."[11] Moltmann reminds us that Christian hope has its origin in the resurrection of Christ, which overpowers the evil revealed supremely in the cross and kindles and renews hope. Therefore, people can rightly "keep their heads up, recognize meaningful goals, and find the courage to invest human and material powers with this purpose."[12]

To find the dream for the church we search the Scriptures, discovering anew God's vision for the world and God's purpose and plan for the church.

The Congregation

What Scripture says about God's vision for the world and plan for the church applies to all congregations, but not always in the same way. Each congregation is unique, with particular histories and needs; therefore each congregation, in accord with its commitments to denominational relationships, considers and decides how it will respond to the vision and call of God.

Answers to questions like the following will help a congregation clarify its vision:

- What is the age profile of the members?
- What are the trends in membership figures?
- What are the trends in worship attendance?
- What are the interests and needs of the members?
- What are their dreams, their hopes?
- What are the program needs?
- What are the stewardship needs?
- What are the facility needs?
- What are the staffing needs?

The vision of the congregation will be shaped in part by the unique features of the congregation, the needs, interests, and longings of its people.

The Community

In addition to the vision of Scripture and the characteristics and hopes of the congregation, it is necessary to consider the particular community in which the congregation exists. What is it like? What are its needs? What are their dreams? Who are the unchurched?

If possible, do a community survey, asking people for their perception of community needs and also what they would be interested in at the church. Responding to such surveys by changing programs or other aspects of church life will strengthen the church's service to the community.

The World at Large

Because we believe that the world is the beneficiary of God's redemptive work, the church's mission includes the whole world. Again, what are the needs and the hopes? Where is the gospel not heard? What should the church do to carry out its ministry with greater effectiveness?

For example, in our time there is need for food in many parts of the world, and there is need for peace throughout the whole world. What can the church do to help the world overcome its problems of poverty and hunger? And what can the church do to help establish and maintain peace? Answers to such questions will influence and shape the vision of the church.

FROM VISION TO ACTION

When the vision is stated and affirmed, it is time to think of ways to express it in the everyday life of the congregation. To some people, this is the wearisome part, the difficult and sometimes mundane part. But try to see it as a spiritual process. It can also bring joy and create new energy. Remember, planning ways to express the vision is planning ways to express the Christian faith through the ministry and mission of the congregation. Planning is a way of giving expression to the dreams and hopes, vision and commitment of the congregation.

Furthermore, there are many beneficial side effects to the planning process. Edward R. Dayton and Ted W. Engstrom mention three in particular.

> First, the process of goal setting and planning can be the task around which people can focus their energies and thus build their relationships. Second, goal setting and planning can enhance communication about the life of the congregation. Third, because goals and plans are events that have not yet happened, they allow time for corrective action as new information and problems are encountered.[13]

Dayton and Engstrom are so convinced of the value of planning that they espouse a startling theory: "The ability of the Holy Spirit to operate within a local church . . . is directly proportional to the amount of planning done."[14] The authors clarify their position by explaining that when people operate on a day-to-day basis they have access to a very limited amount of information; consequently the decisions are made with little information and little consultation. On the other hand, when information is carefully gathered and reviewed, and when plans are carefully made, the members of the group have time for involvement and reaction with one another around the developing plans, modifying them as they deem appropriate. This means, as Dayton and Engstrom see it, that "there is time for reflection, time for reconsideration, time for the Holy Spirit to quietly do His office work."[15]

PLANNING MODELS

Lyle Schaller says that the planning model you choose has a great impact on the outcome. He sees two distinct models, one that focuses on problems and the other on possibilities. Schaller says the first of the two tends to:

- Produce a strong past orientation;
- Encourage pessimism;
- Reinforce an emphasis on remedial approaches;
- Foster a preoccupation with liabilities;
- Encourage scapegoating;
- Produce frustration-stimulated goals.[16]

A more satisfactory model, says Schaller, is one that is based on the congregation's potential. This model also has some predictable outcomes, tending to:

- Produce a strong future orientation;
- Enhance optimism;
- Nurture creativity;
- Build on assets;
- Attract and motivate new members;
- Result in goals in response to unmet needs.[17]

Elsewhere, Schaller explains in greater detail the second of the two models, calling it the "affirm and build" model. He writes:

> I try to use a planning model that (a) has a strong future-orientation built into it, (b) includes an emphasis on outreach, (c) begins by identifying the distinctive resources, strengths, and assets of that particular congregation, (d) encourages agreement on the definition of contemporary reality as the beginning point for planning for tomorrow, (e) causes people to expand their definition of alternative courses of action, and (f) may challenge some stereotypes that no longer are relevant.[18]

SETTING GOALS

Sooner or later all leadership is goal setting. It may be the personal, hands-on setting of goals for the organization or for some part of the organization; or it may be the oversight given to the goal setting of committees or colleagues. It may be a formal process or done informally in the corridor. Whatever the case, leaders engage in goal setting.

An incident in *Alice's Adventures in Wonderland* by Lewis Carroll (New York: Random House, 1946) can motivate us to overcome the resistance we may have to the hard task of setting goals. When Alice asked the Cheshire cat for directions on which way to go, the cat said it depends on where you want to go. And when Alice said she didn't care, the cat explained that then it doesn't matter which way you go.

As the story suggests, goals indicate where you would go, what you would achieve. In order to make good use of the resources, and to work together with effectiveness and in harmony, goals are essential. Without goals it matters little what we do in the present. Our mission and ministry are significant only in light of the goals. In *The Classic Touch*, John K. Clemens and Douglas F. Mayer discuss the importance of having clearly defined goals. Success, they say, "depends on one thing: an almost slavish dedication to a well-defined goal. Look closely at the anatomy of leadership, and you will generally see a near-monomaniacal leader in hot pursuit of an almost palpable objective."[19]

Yet some in the church argue that the church is not a goal-seeking organization. It is enough, they say, to *be* —simply *be*; it is not necessary to *do*. While we appreciate the calling to *be*, and want to celebrate that status, can we rest with that without resorting to what Dietrich Bonhoeffer called "cheap grace"? Our forebears in the faith were blessed at the initiative of God, but a response was called for; they were blessed to be a blessing to others. Furthermore, when the church came to know the grace of Christ it was given the great commission: to go, to baptize, to teach. The commission of Christ becomes, in turn, the mission of the church, a mission that we pursue best through establishing goals.

Words associated with the planning process are used differently, which is another reason some people resist getting involved. Words such as mission, purpose, goal, objective, and plan are used inconsistently in the literature and by leadership people.

Try these working definitions:

Mission and purpose are synonyms. They refer to the big Why? of the organization.

Vision and dream are used interchangeably. They refer to the overall image of the organization's future and picture a future condition that is better than what now exists.

Goals are descriptions of what we want to achieve, the results of our efforts. They can be general and long-range, or they can be specific and short-range. They are rooted in the nature of the organization, but they reflect the present time. They describe what we want to achieve today and tomorrow.

Objectives are sometimes used interchangeably with goals. Think of them as minigoals, as a way of breaking down the pursuit of the goals into manageable steps. Objectives are what must be accomplished in order to reach the goals.

Action plans are the activities undertaken to meet the objectives and thereby achieve the goals that were set. Action plans are specific, temporary, and vital.

Is it necessary to include all of the components in the planning process? Not always; not in small organizations that are relatively simple in structure.

I suggest four parts (Figure 14).

MISSION ⟶ VISION ⟶ GOALS ⟶ ACTION PLAN

Figure 14

The *mission*, remember, is to participate in God's redemptive purpose. The *vision* may be to build a congregation that is responsive to God's word and promise, compassionate toward the poor, evangelical toward the unchurched, joyful in its calling. A *goal* could be, for example, to increase the baptized membership by 50 during the current year. And the *action plan* will detail the necessary steps to take in order to achieve the goal.

For many people the goals are the hardest to develop. One reason is that before you can state your goals you have to think clearly and carefully about what it is you want to achieve. In other words, you have to make decisions and commitments. Also, the goals must be specific. If not, your goal statements are abstract and deserve to be called "fuzzies."

Robert F. Mager suggests the Hey Dad Test for developing and writing goals statements. Finish this sentence with your intended goal and see how it sounds: Hey Dad, let me show you how I can . . . If the result sounds absurd, you are most likely dealing with an abstraction—an unsatisfactory goal. Try this one: Hey Dad, watch me bring in the kingdom. Or this one: Hey Dad, watch me understand Paul. Both are abstractions, fuzzies that reflect inadequate goals. On the other hand, you could develop your statements like this: Hey Dad, watch me lead a Bible study on the kingdom of God as expressed in Matthew. Hey Dad, watch me read this book on the life of St. Paul. The latter two will pass the Hey Dad Test.[20]

Here are some additional things to keep in mind when determining goals. They must be:

- In harmony with the mission;
- Reasonably possible to attain;
- Measurable;
- Understandable.

When writing a goal statement begin with the word "to," followed by an active verb.

Some people find it helpful to set goals for many of the church's ministries, setting membership goals, attendance goals, program goals. While not everyone wants to be that detailed in goal setting, it is worth remembering that goals can significantly influence the effectiveness of the ministry. Dayton and Engstrom speak of "the awesome power of goals," and when you reflect on what they say goals can accomplish, you are apt to agree. Goals:

- Give a sense of direction and purpose;
- Give us the power to live in the present;
- Promote enthusiasm and strong organizational life;
- Help us to operate effectively;

- Help us to evaluate progress;
- Help us plan ahead;
- Help us communicate within the organization;
- Give people a clear understanding of what is expected;
- Help to reduce needless conflict and duplication of effort;
- Take the emphasis off activity and place it on output.[21]

THE ACTION PLAN

As indicated, goals declare what we intend to achieve. They are the target, the outcome, the results. But how do we get there? What do we do in order to reach the goals we have set? The answer to that is our strategy, or, as I prefer, our action plan.

For example, suppose you set a membership goal for your church as follows: To increase our baptized membership by 50 people by the end of the year. Does it pass the Hey Dad Test? Yes. Hey Dad, watch us grow by 50 members!

The next step is to decide what to do in order to reach that goal—that is, to develop the action plan. You might come up with a list of such things as these:

- Contact visitors to our church within one week of their visit.
- Train 12 members to call on the unchurched in the neighborhood.
- Sponsor a friendship Sunday, encouraging members to bring friends to church.
- Run weekly ads in the paper.
- Conduct a neighborhood survey to determine interests, needs, and church affiliation.

The action plan should be very specific. It is wise to state the dates by which the steps will be completed, and to state who is the responsible person or group. Goals may have great power, but only if there is a plan of action carried out in a timely manner. While it is important to plan your work, it is also important to work your plan. This is what an action plan invites you to do.

Alvin Lindgren and Norman Shawchuck have adapted a poem that is a fitting conclusion to this chapter.

There once was preacher
Whose principle feature
Was hidden in quite an odd way.
    Lay persons by millions
    Or possibly zillions
    Surrounded him all of the day.

When once seen
By his saintly bishop
And asked how he managed the deed,
    He lifted three fingers
    And said, "All you swingers
    Need only follow my lead."

To rise from a zero
To a big parish hero
To answer these questions you'll strive:
    Where are we going,
    How will we get there, and
    How will we know we've arrived?[22]

12

MOTIVATING

The authors of the widely read book *In Search of Excellence* conclude that people want more than profit for their efforts, more than salary increases and benefits. People seek meaning, they say. The source of meaning is shared commitment to excellence in product and service.[1]

The issue here is the subject of this chapter—motivation, the wellspring of action.

Motivation is no simple subject. Our motives are rooted in our needs, some of them conscious and some unconscious. To make things more complex, some of our needs are physical while others are emotional. The need for air, water, food, sex, sleep, and shelter are all physical. The more ambiguous, emotional needs include self-esteem, affection, affiliation, aspirations, and expectations.

Everything we do, good or bad, effective or ineffective, painful or pleasurable, is to satisfy the powerful forces within called needs. In the church we face an especially complex challenge when it comes to motivating people.

- The members are all volunteers.
- The two major goals are in tension with each other, sometimes in conflict:
  —to nurture and build up the membership;
  —to equip people for service to others.
- The membership is made up of anyone who confesses faith in Christ, regardless of other qualifications.

Despite the complexity of the entire subject, a key to leadership is the way in which leaders respond to their followers' needs. Genuine leadership is inseparable from followers' needs.

SOME APPROACHES
NOT RECOMMENDED

The complexity of motivation sometimes leads to approaches that leave much to be desired.

One of these is motivation through guilt. While guilt is a powerful motive and is used with some regularity in the church, the longer-term consequences indicate that it is best to avoid the use of guilt as a motive. One of the side effects of guilt is avoidance—people tend to shy away from those who make them feel guilty. Another side effect is passiveness. This often follows the usually temporary flurry of activity that may be produced by guilt, and leaves the inner person unchanged except for negative feelings.

Another approach not recommended is to motivate through fear. While the "fear of the Lord" may well be the beginning of wisdom, the fear we are concerned with here is not that which holds God in reverence or awe, but which threatens punishment. As a motive, fear prompts action that reduces the fear, not action that pursues a goal. Fear may even immobilize those it seeks to move. Of course some fear is necessary and may have a purpose; children, for example, need to know what will happen to them if they run into a busy street. Fear should not be ruled out as an appropriate motive to tap under any and all circumstances, but it belongs near the bottom of the list. It is generally an approach not recommended.

A third approach not recommended is motivation through manipulation. It comes in many disguises—from telling half-truths to deceiving another into believing falsehoods for his or her own good. Manipulation is getting a person to do something when, if that person knew what was happening, he or she would at least have serious misgivings. It is often the attempt to use or influence persons for the advantage of someone else. In short, manipulation is a dishonest mistreatment of people. And when manipulated, people appropriately feel alienated from the person or organization that is responsible.

RESPONDING TO NEEDS

The better approach to motivation is to respond to the needs of people. True leaders take seriously the needs of their followers and, in turn, the needs of the society and larger world.

Human needs can be summarized under three headings: survival, satisfaction, and self-actualization. Behind all the varied behaviors of people is the expression of one or the other of these three inclusive needs, and often a combination of two or more.

The survival need is the drive to maintain one's self, the drive to stay alive. In general, this refers to the physical needs mentioned above—the need for food, air, water, and shelter. It has to do with concern for wellness, for pay raises, possibly for faith in Christ who promised, "I will come again and take you to myself" (John 14:3).

The need for satisfaction is the need to find enjoyment and pleasure in life. Fulfillment of this need is sought in numerous ways—from eating good food, to enjoying friends and family, to attending movies, to hearing sermons in church. As we grow and mature we seek the fulfillment of the need for pleasure and satisfaction in different ways, for our interests change, as do our values and ambitions.

The self-actualization need is the drive to find meaning and fulfillment in life. Again, fulfillment is sought in different ways, depending on a person's interests and opportunities. One person may take classes at a college or university, another may read the Greek philosophers, while still others may work with the homeless, run for political office, take dancing lessons, develop a more active prayer life, or participate in church activities.

The relationships between the three basic needs are not simple. They overlap; they are intertwined; sometimes they are at cross-purposes. For example, drinking a malted milk meets both survival and satisfaction needs; attending church may meet both satisfaction and self-actualization needs; earning money, especially when some of it is used to help the poor, may meet aspects of all three needs. Also, one need can be expressed through several different interests, and several needs can be expressed in one interest or activity.

With this overview of motivational theory as background, we now pause to consider several schools of thought on the subject, each of which is associated with the name of the person who developed the theory.

MASLOW'S HIERARCHY OF NEEDS

In the mid-fifties psychologist Abraham Maslow developed a theory of human motivation, based not on a study of troubled or sick people but on a study of the healthiest, most adequate men and women he could find—people who seemed close to fulfilling their potential.

Maslow concluded that our many needs are hierarchical in nature, that is, some take precedence over others, and that these must be met before those higher on the scale come into play. Maslow's various needs can be arranged in hierarchical order like steps on a staircase (Figure 15).[2]

The physical and safety needs are what were referred to earlier as survival needs. The need for belonging moves us into the emotional category, from the survival mode into the satisfaction mode. The need for esteem is one reason why people excel on the job or write books, and for most it is higher on the scale than that of belonging. Self-actualization gets at the quest for meaning in life. It is followed by the need for intellectual understanding and the drive for aesthetic enjoyment. While the various needs

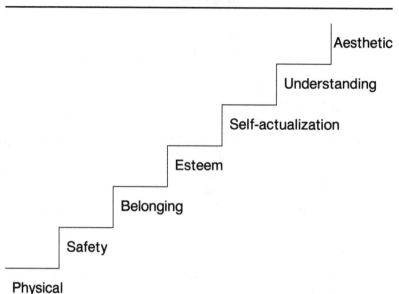

Figure 15

are intertwined, Maslow said those that are lower on the staircase must be met before the higher ones have significant power.

When you seek to motivate people you will want to know where they are on the scale of needs. If you aim too low, your message will seem redundant, for those needs are already met. If you aim too high, your message will seem irrelevant, for the people aren't aware of such needs. Also, note the following premises:[3]

- The closer the need is to the bottom of the hierarchy, the more power it exerts over a person's actions.
- We are forever in need; needs are insatiable.
- When a need is satisfied, albeit temporarily, it is no longer a motivator.
- We expend our energy to meet our needs.
- Functioning at the higher levels of need reflects growth and maturity.

HERZBERG'S MOTIVATION-HYGIENE THEORY

Psychologist Frederick Herzberg takes Maslow's hierarchy of needs another step by distinguishing between motivators and de-motivators, calling them satisfiers and dissatisfiers. In his research Herzberg discovered that the factors that make people happy with their jobs are not the opposite of those that make them unhappy. In other words, removing the dissatisfiers results only in less dissatisfaction, not more satisfaction.

What are the satisfiers and the dissatisfiers? Herzberg lists five of each.[4]

Satisfiers	Dissatisfiers
Achievement	Interpersonal relationships
Recognition	Supervision
Challenging work	Company policy/administration
Increased responsibility	Working conditions
Growth and advancement	Money, status, security

According to Herzberg, the dissatisfiers have to do with the environment of a person's work or activity. Changing them changes only the degree of dissatisfaction, and has nothing to do with the satisfaction level of the people, nor with their motivation or lack of it. The degree of satisfaction a person experiences is determined by the items in the satisfiers column. These, then, are the motivators, for they appeal to the needs of people. Leaders who are most successful seek ways of increasing experiences listed in the satisfiers column.

McCLELLAND'S NEED THEORY

David C. McClelland contributed to the understanding of motivation by identifying three types of basic motivating needs—achievement, power, and affiliation.[5]

The need for achievement, obviously stronger in some people than in others, is seen in the concern for excellence in performance of all kinds. Success is marked by excellent or at least by improved performance.

The need for power is reflected in the desire to influence others, to have an impact on their lives or on the world as a whole. Power here is not to be seen in a negative light, for the need to have an impact is just as worthy as the need to achieve.

The need for affiliation is the need for good relationships with colleagues and groups. Those with strong affiliation needs are usually considered to be people-oriented, and emphasize not the achievement of the group or its impact but the relationships that result.

McClelland's views not only help us understand more about the complex subject of motivation; they provide a way to look at an organization as a whole. The church, for example, wants to achieve its mission, wants to be of influence in people's lives and in the world at large, and wants to be a place where affiliation needs are met. Some in the church will respond more readily to one need expression and others to another but, taken as a whole, the church will seek to provide fulfillment experiences for all three of the needs. In turn, it will fulfill its own motives of achievement, power, and affiliation.

VICTOR VROOM'S EXPECTANCY THEORY

Psychologist Victor Vroom has developed quite a different theory of motivation, which is commonly called the "expectancy theory."[6] The central point of this theory is that if people believe their actions will help achieve certain goals, they will be motivated to take the necessary actions.

Vroom suggests that a person's motivation for an action at any time is determined by his or her anticipated values of both negative and positive outcomes (Figure 16).

FORCE = VALENCE × EXPECTANCY

Figure 16

Force is the strength of a person's motivation. Valence is the strength of a person's preference for an outcome, and expectancy is the person's perception of the probability that a particular action will lead to a desired outcome. If the expectancy is zero or negative there is no motivation to achieve the goal; similarly, there is no motivation if the valence is zero or negative. The force exerted to do something depends upon both valence and expectancy. Our motivation is high when the valence and expectancy are positive and high.

One of the attractive features of Vroom's expectancy theory is that it recognizes the presence of varied individual needs and motivations. Moreover, it is compatible with the emphasis on goal-orientation prominent in many of today's organizations and churches, and the task-orientation of many leaders.

This quick survey of the key motivational theories not only indicates something of the complexity of human motivation and behavior but also emphasizes how motivation both depends on and influences leadership style. The last word on the subject has obviously not been spoken, yet it is clear that leaders in today's world are obliged to pay careful attention to the needs of people—as varied, fluctuating, and erratic as they may be—if they want reasonable success and satisfaction in their leadership roles.

IF WE WANT PEOPLE TO DO THEIR BEST

The following list reflects many of the theories we have considered and gives practical application to people in volunteer organizations, the church included. If we want them to do their best, they:

- Need to know what is going to happen to them as persons, what will be expected of them, and how their contributions will fit into the group.
- Need a sense of belonging, a feeling that no one objects to their presence, a feeling that they are sincerely welcome, a feeling that they are wanted for their total self.
- Need to have a share in planning the group goals and the confidence that the goals are within reach.

- Need to have responsibilities that challenge and yet are within range of their abilities—and that contribute to the achievement of the group goals.
- Need to see that progress is being made toward the goals of the organization.
- Need to have confidence in the leadership of the group, with assurance that the leaders will be fair as well as competent, trustworthy, and loyal.
- Need at any given time to conclude: "This situation makes sense to me."[7]

MOTIVATION AND TRANSFORMING LEADERS

In chapter 2 we considered the two leadership approaches suggested by James MacGregor Burns: transactional and transforming. To Burns, most leaders spend most of their time with transactional issues, focusing on the everyday activities and concerns, the means and not the ends of the organization. Burns goes on to point out the values and opportunities of transforming leadership—the kind "that raises the level of human conduct and ethical aspiration of both leader and led, and thus . . . has a transforming effect upon both."[8]

Burns knows that leaders must acknowledge the needs of people. Indeed, his definition of leadership includes such acknowledgment when he states:

> I define leadership as leaders inducing followers to act for certain goals that represent the values and the motivations—the wants and needs, the aspirations and expectations—of both leaders and followers. And the genius of leadership lies in the manner in which leaders see and act on their own and their followers' values and motivations.[9]

Yet Burns does not imply that the motivations of people are what they could or should be. He argues that they can be changed, and that such is the leaders' opportunity and responsibility, using transforming leadership.

Leaders can also shape and alter and elevate the motives and values and goals of followers through the vital teaching role of leadership. This is transforming leadership. The premise of this leadership is that, whatever the separate interests persons might hold, they are presently or potentially united in the pursuit of "higher" goals, the realization of which is tested by the achievement of significant change that represents the collective or pooled interests of leaders and followers.[10]

Burns quotes John Gardner on the moral leadership that leaders are in a position to give:

They can express the values that hold the society together. Most important, they can conceive and articulate goals that lift people out of their petty preoccupations, carry them above the conflicts that tear a society apart, and unite them in the pursuit of objectives worthy of their best efforts.[11]

Presumably, says Burns, one can lead others downward—"down the primrose path or down the road to barbarism. Yet leadership has the connotation of leading people upward, to some higher value or purpose or form of self-fulfillment."[12]

In view of what Burns and Gardner and others have said, it would seem especially appropriate for church leaders to forthrightly advocate the values of the faith—shaping, altering, and elevating the values and goals that people currently embrace.

For example, church leaders can teach gratitude—knowing not only that it is a basic motive for Christian living but also that it is a higher value that people are able to achieve through teaching and growth.

Also, church leaders can teach responsibility—linking it to the faithfulness and obedience that is urged in the Scripture and to the calling of God into a covenant relationship of blessing and service.

And church leaders can teach love, clarifying that it is finally rooted in God's love and showing how it is related to power and justice.

Moreover, when considering motivation theory and practice, it is appropriate to acknowledge that faith may well be the most powerful motivator of all. People of faith are motivated by God's word of grace and promise, by the presence of the Spirit, and by the freedom to respond to God's commandments to love and serve others. People of faith respond to the call to be "doers of the word" and are motivated to express that call in a variety of ways.

WHAT MOTIVATES YOU?

Our motives are complex, usually mixed, often elusive. Yet, in order to lead and be of influence, as well as to understand ourselves, it is helpful to be aware of the prevailing motives in our various involvements. The following exercise can be helpful for individual or group use.

Factors That Motivate

Indicate the five items that you believe are the most important in motivating you (or that account for your participation in this group). Note the key at the end of the chapter.

1. _____ I enjoy it; it is interesting.
2. _____ Others are doing it.
3. _____ It leads to recognition from others.
4. _____ It is easy.
5. _____ I feel the task is important.
6. _____ I have the skill to do it.
7. _____ I feel trusted and respected in it.
8. _____ I have the opportunity to do a good job.
9. _____ I will be disciplined if I don't do it.
10. _____ I have a chance to help with the planning.
11. _____ I get along well with others at the task.
12. _____ I have the opportunity to take responsibility.
13. _____ I have a large amount of freedom doing it.
14. _____ I have a good supervisor or leader.
15. _____ I have the opportunity to grow and develop.

16. ____ I have the opportunity to meet others.
17. ____ I have the opportunity to earn money.
18. ____ There are good rewards offered.
19. ____ Other: _____ [13]

People seek meaning, say the authors of In Search of Excellence. In addition to salary increases and other benefits, they seek the meaning that is realized through commitment to excellence in product and service. In the church such commitments have an added dimension—the glory of God, God's call to discipleship and service, the assurance that in the Lord our labor in never in vain.

Key to Factors that Motivate

The list of motivations fall into three general categories:
• Personal rewards or satisfactions: 1, 4, 6, 9, 13, 17, 18.
• Enjoyment of being with others: 2, 3, 7, 11, 14, 16.
• Satisfactions from worthwhile activity: 5, 8, 10, 12, 15.

It is helpful to know your primary motivations. It will also help your supervisor assign you to the most satisfying activity.

13

MANAGING
CONFLICT

The church is no stranger to conflict. The disciples of Christ quarreled about places in the kingdom and about the best way to do the work of God. And when push came to shove, one of them was a traitor to the entire cause.

Jesus assumed there would be conflict among his followers and gave instructions on how to respond:

> If your brother sins against you, go and tell him his fault, between you and him alone. If he listens to you, you have gained your brother. But if he does not listen, take one or two others along with you, that every word may be confirmed by the evidence of two or three witnesses. If he refuses to listen to them, tell it to the church; and if he refuses to listen even to the church, let him be to you as a Gentile and a tax collector.
>
> (Matt. 18:15–17)

The apostle Paul was distressed with the church at Corinth not because there was conflict but because they resorted to the use of secular courts to resolve the conflict (1 Cor. 6:1–6). Paul was himself at the center of conflict; not only with the secular authorities but also with his brothers and sisters in the faith. With his colleagues he was contentious and argumentative, and his sharp disagreement with Barnabas led to a parting of their ways (Acts 15:36–41).

Conflict is a major issue in the world, as the continuing arms race, international tensions, and the breakdown of marriage and family would all indicate.

Conflict is also a serious issue in the church, if not among the rank and file, then among the leaders and would-be leaders. Conflict seems to happen wherever people care deeply about something.

IS CONFLICT ALWAYS HARMFUL?

To most people, conflict is a negative experience, disrupting and painful. Conflict is to be avoided—perhaps even at all costs. Some would point out, however, that conflict is good, or at least potentially good. They would point to the worldwide concern for justice as an example of how temporary conflict can lead to greater good. It can be argued, too, that conflict stimulates interest and activity, that it serves as a safety valve for hostilities, that it prompts change and that it strengthens the human character.

However, these arguments ought not be emphasized to the neglect of the harmful effects of conflict. For while some good can come of conflict—just as some good can come of tragedy—the potential for harm must be faced as well. Conflict can make people feel defeated and demeaned, can generate distrust and disillusionment, can produce apathy and alienation. The potential for harm would suggest the importance of taking whatever conflict-prevention steps are possible. As G. W. Garvin discovered in his research on growing churches, skill and openness in managing conflict is one of four principles critical to church growth.[1]

Yet the positive evaluation of conflict made by educator David Bandey is intriguing:

> Life is essentially and not accidently the operation of reconciliation on conflict, of healing on illness, of forgiveness on guilt, of love on

enmity. It is not a state of harmony; it is an act of harmonizing chaos, disorder, anarchy, strife, and all other negations of creativity that are continually there and continually being overcome. . . .

We can say that the anarchic negations in life are opposed by the creativity of redemption or salvific action, through the operation of the Spirit, who is the life-giver.

Jesus was not a desperate remedy applied by God to a world which had got out of hand. Anselm rightly contended that God is not one who can be driven into a corner by conditions within his own creation. Jesus was the presence of God in the world as it is. We experience the presence of God not as being but as act. . . .

I am not arguing that conflict is good-in-itself, or that in an absolute and eternal sense it ought to be . . . but spiritual life develops in the conflict against spiritual chaos, which is encountered as evil.[2]

Martin Marty, who included the above quotation in an issue of *Context*, says that in Bandey's view conflict situations surround us as invitations, not exclusions—even as manifestations of the works of God and opportunities for incarnation. While that may be an encouraging word to hear, we nevertheless should seek to prevent conflict whenever possible and work to minimize its negative aspects.

WHAT CAUSES CONFLICT?

To prevent conflict, as well as to manage it once it has come, it is helpful to know some things about its source. We identify and examine briefly five causes of conflict.

Personalities

In the last chapter we considered three different categories of people in terms of their needs or primary motivations. Some are interested in affiliation, some in achievement, some in power. The differences can be the source of conflict, for the values and goals of each are different.

For example, affiliation people are relationship-oriented and tend to put relationships first. This can result in conflict with people whose interest is achievement and also with those who value making an impact, the power-oriented people.

Under the heading of "personalities," we also acknowledge the frequent presence of what Kenneth Haugk and William McKay call "parish antagonists"—people who are chronic in their criticisms of the pastor and other leaders, and whose attack is almost always based on rumor, half-truths, or unsubstantiated charges and allegations. Parish antagonists are often vindictive and their influence is usually harmful to the congregation as a whole.[3] Peg Meier sees three different types of such difficult people, common in a variety of social or work groups: the "tanks" who are aggressive and direct in their attack; the "snipes" who are hit-and-run specialists; and the "clams" who silently withdraw from all activity.[4]

Nature of the Church

The church's two basic goals—to nurture and serve the members and to reach out to the world—are often in tension with each other. And people often tend to line up with one or the other, advocating support for missions over program, or vice versa, and promoting for leadership positions those who they feel will emphasize their favorite projects. Some of the conflict is therefore rooted in the basic nature of the church.

Role Confusion

This is usually between the pastor and the elected leadership of the congregation. It is a common problem in general administrative responsibilities. Some lay leaders want the pastor to take a more assertive leadership role, a role that the pastor may or may not want to assume. Others want the pastor to back away from leadership responsibilities, seeing him or her as comparable to a hospital chaplain with little or no administrative responsibilities. When the pastor does not affirm or assume the role advocated by the lay leaders, the result is often conflict.

Inadequate Structure

The decision-making process may be such that people get in each other's way. The documents may be unclear or nonexistent.

160

There may be no established personnel policies for the staff, which means that fair and equitable treatment is unlikely. Committees may know neither the scope nor extent of their responsibilities. Staff members may be without position descriptions, a situation that often results in unclear or conflicting expectations. In short, the structure of the organization is such that conflict is unavoidable.

Inadequate Communication

Marriage counselors maintain that communication is the lifeline of the marriage relationship. The same can be said for an organization—communication is the lifeline, the means of conveying information, which in turn helps the members of the organization remain committed as well as informed. But sometimes this is neglected, communication breaks down or is simply nonexistent, and members begin to feel left out and uninformed. In time, misunderstandings creep in. Misinformation is carried through the grapevine; people become restive and dissatisfied. Inadequate or unclear communication produces a situation ripe for conflict.

What has been your experience of conflict? Here is a checklist that will help an individual or group diagnose their own conflict experience.[5]

CHECKLIST FOR DIAGNOSING CONFLICTS

Instructions: Indicate whether you agree or disagree with each of the statements, and then turn to the end of the chapter for the interpretation.

1. _____ Most conflicts with superiors occur over facts.
2. _____ Most conflicts with subordinates occur over perceptions.
3. _____ Most conflicts with peers occur over role positions.
4. _____ Getting correct information is enough to resolve most conflicts.
5. _____ Most conflicts evolve through stages.
6. _____ The more managers know about each other, the more likely it is that they will have conflicts.
7. _____ Avoiding small differences is often the best approach.

8. ____ It is seldom a good idea to directly confront your superiors about a disagreement.
9. ____ You can work effectively with people you disagree with.
10. ____ In a conflict, understanding each other is often more important than agreeing with each other.

PREVENTING CONFLICT

While not all conflict in the church can be prevented, there are preventive measures that can reduce the amount and degree of conflict. Consider the following suggestions in response to the causes of conflict that were listed.

Deal With the Personality Issues

When we deepen our understanding of human nature and behavior, our expectations of people are more realistic. The list of motivating needs identified by David McClelland, introduced in the last chapter and referred to above—affiliation, achievement and power—is a helpful reminder that not all people are alike. This fact calls not only for understanding, but for tolerance and flexibility as well.

What about the parish antagonists? Should they be allowed to do whatever they will? Haugk and McKay say no. While patience is called for, and while attempts must be made to understand the antagonist's views, the time may come when the antagonist should be asked to cease and desist or leave the congregation. If the congregation's harmony and mission are being hampered, such a drastic step is warranted.

Cecil Osborne, the founder of Yokefellows, Inc. and author of *The Art of Getting Along With People*, takes an even more forthright stand. He writes: "We have an obligation to try to straighten people out, but if they refuse to change, we must rid the church of their presence and influence."[6]

Troublemakers, says Osborne, should be reminded of the qualifications of church membership, which include promoting the peace and harmony of the church. When they continue to stir up

the church with rumors, gossip, and speculation they are in viola-
tion of one of the congregation's principles. So they should be
called before the board of deacons to explain themselves and to
again qualify. If they are unwilling to do so, they should be dis-
missed from membership, says Osborne. He adds, "We have no
moral, theological, or ecclesiastical right to leave people like that
in our churches."[7]

Keep the Church Balanced

To avoid the conflict that is rooted in the nature and twofold
purpose of the church, be intentional in maintaining balance in the
overall ministry—in preaching and teaching, in setting the goals,
and in determining the budget. Some say that the purpose of the
church is to reach the unchurched. This position deserves to be
called "ecclesiastical hyperbole," a way of hyping the missions or
evangelism programs of the church, even to the neglect of its other
programs and ministries. Others would say that we are sending too
much of our money to missions, that we need to fix the roof, carpet
the floor, and hire somebody to work with the youth. This is a
nuts-and-bolts way of saying that charity begins at home. Is the
church to nurture its own, or is it to reach out to the unchurched
and the needy? The answer is, obviously, both. Balanced ministries
of preaching, teaching, and congregational life that honor the
church's twofold purpose will help avoid the conflict that is rooted
in an inadequate theology and image of the church.

Clear Up Role Confusion

Review the constitution and other official documents of the
congregation, including the pastor's letter of call, to see what they
say about the roles of the leaders. Think through and talk over
the subject until there is a common understanding, making necessary clarifications. And see that the staff members have clearly
written descriptions of their responsibilities, including to whom
each is accountable. More than one congregation has put a stop to
its conflict by stating in the bylaws of the constitution that all staff
are accountable to the pastor or his or her designate.

Bring Decision-Making and Operating Procedures to Proper Order

Review the official documents from this perspective, too. Some documents clearly state the procedures while others require revisions. The role and responsibilities of the congregational council and the various committees should be detailed. For additional insights on this subject, turn back to chapters 8, 9, and 10. Cecil Osborne, quoted above, maintains that by rewriting the constitution one church got rid of 50 percent of the potential for conflict in the congregation.[8]

Improve Communication

Ours is an "information society," says John Naisbitt in *Megatrends.* But long before we were described in that way leaders had the responsibility to communicate with their followers.

Information about goals and program plans is essential. Information about needs and opportunities is also essential. An informed person is usually an interested person; an informed person is usually challenged toward deeper commitment and involvement; an informed person is less inclined to produce conflict and more inclined to bring a spirit of harmony.

Use of the following questions, received at a Robert Schuller seminar on church leadership, will strengthen communication and reduce the chances of conflict.

- *Disarming questions:* Do you feel I can help you solve this problem?
- *Bridge-building questions:* I'd like to help you. Why don't we try to solve this problem together?
- *Questions that foster understanding:* I'm sure you have many good reasons for thinking the way you do. But since I don't see it your way, won't you share them with me?
- *Truth-revealing questions:* You seem to be better informed than I. Where and when did you get this information?
- *Tolerance-producing questions:* I still see another side to this. May I share my thoughts on this with you?

- *Questions that may point up your opponent's weaknesses and disadvantages:* Do you see any dangers that could arise if we followed your suggestions?
- *Questions that put your opponents in your shoes:* What would you do if you were in my position?
- *Questions that create an atmosphere for compromise negotiation:* What, as you see it, are the alternatives? Could we ask someone else for an opinion?
- *Questions that beg for time:* If what you say is correct we will have to take the time to reexamine our policy (or attitude or position). Let me study your findings so that we can get together soon to explore various solutions.

CONFLICT COMES ON DIFFERENT LEVELS

Speed Leas, director of counseling at the Alban Institute, is widely known for his research and writing on the subject of conflict in the church. In one of his writings he identifies five different levels of conflict, determined by what seem to be the objectives of the participants and by the language they use.

Level One. At this level the conflict is seen as a problem to solve, and the participants are able to focus on the problem. Language is specific and clear.

Level Two. On this level people become more self-protective. The problem now becomes secondary, while the participants protect themselves. Language will be general and often not specifically about an issue.

Level Three. Here people turn from self-protection and take the offensive. They are concerned now with winning, with having their views prevail. They read minds, distort, talk about perceptions as if they were facts.

Level Four. The objective again changes. No longer are the people interested in merely winning; they want to get rid of someone. There has to be a parting of the ways. Language becomes even more distorted.

Level Five. On this level people become religious fanatics about their position, and may even feel called by God to save the church by getting rid of the pastor. The pastor must not simply resign and leave; if he or she is called by another congregation, that congregation must be warned.[9]

Leas states that problem-solving techniques are usually helpful in levels one through three, but that outside help is needed for levels four and five. For his own work as a conflict management consultant, he sets four goals.

One: Help people define the decisions they can make.

Two: Help people join in decision-making processes that are fair and legal.

Three: Reduce tension in the organization.

Four: Help people learn from the conflict.

NEGOTIATION IS ALWAYS GOOD

Roger Fisher and William Ury, the authors of *Getting to Yes,* are members of the Harvard Negotiation Project at Harvard University, a group that deals continually with all levels of conflict resolution from domestic to business to international disputes. In their popular book they propose a four-step method of conflict resolution:

1. *Separate the people from the problem.* Deal with the people as people, and with the problem as the problem. "Dealing with a substantive problem and maintaining a good working relationship need not be conflicting goals if the parties are committed and psychologically prepared to treat each separately on its own merits," say Fisher and Ury.[10]

2. *Focus on the interests, not the positions.* Interests are the desires and concerns of the people, the silent movers behind the position. The position is what they decided would satisfy the interests. "Reconciling interests rather than compromising between positions also works because behind opposed positions lie many more interests than conflicting ones."[11]

3. *Invent options for mutual gain.* Often people in conflict think in terms of a win/lose situation, or, as Fisher and Ury

would say, in terms of a fixed pie. By inventing options, through brainstorming and creative thought, people begin to see other possibilities, see that it can be a win/win situation. Fisher and Ury write, "In a complex situation, creative inventing is an absolute necessity. In any negotiation it may open doors and produce a range of potential agreements satisfactory to each side. Therefore, generate many options before selecting among them. Invent first; decide later. Look for shared interests and differing interests to dovetail. And seek to make their decision easy."[12]

4. *Insist on using objective criteria.* In determining the price of a used car, for example, you can appropriately refer to the "blue book," at least as a starting place. A realtor will show what comparable houses in the neighborhood have sold for. Whatever the issue being negotiated, look for objective criteria of some sort. "If trying to settle differences of interest on the basis of will has such high costs, the solution is to negotiate on some basis *independent* of the will of either side—that is, on the basis of objective criteria," say Fisher and Ury.[13]

HANDLING EVERYDAY CONFLICT ISSUES

Leas, Fisher, and Ury provide us with insights and strategies for coping with various levels of conflict. Their views are rooted in research and experience, and can be useful in many different settings, both in the church and in secular organizations.

Is there a less complicated approach, one that can help us handle many of the everyday conflict experiences without getting side-tracked from our mission? Consider this five-step formula:

One, be assertive enough to express your views, your frustrations, dissatisfactions, and pains. A word of caution, however: Do it in the right time and the right place.

Two, acknowledge your own part in the problem. Confess your participation, your shortcomings, your desire to see change.

Three, be willing to work at it. Set aside time, think and pray about the problem. The solution may not be what you prefer but be satisfied with a solution you can support.

Four, think reconciliation. This is the approach Jesus urged. Forgiveness, acceptance, and right relationships are Christian values to affirm and to move toward.

Five, remember that our primary commitment is the cause of Christ. Sometimes our other commitments and concerns must be put on hold or even surrendered for the sake of the gospel.

Interpretation of the checklist. Most authorities would agree with statements 2, 5, 9, 10. They would tend to disagree with statements 1, 3, 4, 6, 7, 8. Nine of 10 correct is excellent; 7 or 8 is good; 6 or less is average or above.

14

COORDINATING, ORGANIZING, AND STAFFING

In previous chapters we considered such key leadership tasks as planning, motivating, and conflict management. In this chapter we examine three more: coordinating, organizing, and staffing. These, too, are among the everyday tasks of leaders, and each contributes to the well-being and mission of the church.

COORDINATING

Coordination is the synchronization of group effort, assuring that the various parts are properly timed and correct in both quantity and quality. The work of coordination can be thought of as orchestration—bringing harmony and balance to the life of the group, thus making the best use of the available gifts, while reflecting the harmonizing influence of God's redemptive work in the world.

Consider five principles of coordination:

Accountability. The church sees itself as a responsible community, responding in an answerable way to God, self, and neighbor. Because the church is a responsible community, it views its life and work seriously and is concerned that its efforts are useful and productive. The principle of accountability ought to inform all of the church's life. Coordination helps the church fulfill this concern for accountability.

Interdependency. As already indicated, the church is like a system with many parts, none of which functions independently. This also corresponds to Paul's image of the church, the body of Christ with many members, each serving the welfare of the whole. In the Evangelical Church in America, for example, the congregations, synods, and church at large are committed to the organizational principle summed up in the word "interdependency." The work of coordination in the church involves the leaders in seeing that the principle of interdependency is acknowledged and honored.

Balance. A church without balance cannot effectively carry out its mission. Out of balance, it focuses on one or more aspects of mission to the neglect of the whole. The principle of balance will see that there is balance between the church's inner and outer life—with some of the resources being directed toward building up the inner life of the church and some of it going toward the mission of the church beyond itself. Internally, too, the principle of balance is to be honored. If both worship and education are valid ministries, for example, then sufficient resources must be allocated to both. Each ministry of the congregation, valid in light of the congregation's goals, is allocated the resources it needs. This expresses the balancing aspect of coordination.

Communication. This is a practical necessity as well as a principle of coordination. The right hand must know what the left hand is doing. Communication is the lifeline of relationships and organizations. There must be a free flow of information between the various groups and committees. The life of a church can be properly coordinated only if there is adequate and effective communication.

Participation. A prominent feature of life in today's world is the desire of people to participate in the affairs that affect their lives. This is especially appropriate in the church, for the ministry and mission belong to the church as a whole, not only to the leaders.

170

The work of coordination encourages participation by seeing that the resources of time and talent are used constructively.

There are different ways of improving the coordination of a church's ministries. One way is to emphasize the overall purpose and goals of the congregation, asking and urging that each group or committee clarify its own goals and program its activities in light of those that exist for the congregation as a whole. Another way to strengthen coordination is to improve the relationships within and between the various groups. Still another is to train the leaders in more effective leadership and motivational skills. Each of these approaches can make important contributions to the overall task of coordination. But another ingredient is necessary—coordination must be built into the very structure of the organization.

ORGANIZING

This is the general process of structuring a community for its life and work. To organize is to make whatever arrangements are necessary so that the resources of the group are brought to bear on its purpose and goals.

From the beginning this has been a concern in the church. The apostle Paul wrote letters to the churches not only to encourage and instruct them in the faith, but also to instruct them in how to organize themselves. On one occasion he concluded an extended section on the relationship between spiritual gifts and church order by saying, "All things should be done decently and in order" (1 Cor. 14:40).

Gibson Winter states that the task of organizing the church and its work is actually a mark of seriousness about itself and its mission:

One way we distinguish the commonsense world of everyday life from dreaming, fantasy, and aesthetic enjoyment is by the degree of organization expected in our activities and responses. We do not expect dreams to manifest their contents in highly organized forms. Many dreams seem to reorder haphazardly the basic theme of everyday life. Organization means a rational ordering of various elements and phases directed toward the effective realization of an anticipated state of affairs.[1]

As important as organization may be, we do not believe that God has revealed how to organize the church. As Winter continues: "Protestantism takes a pragmatic view of organization. As long as agencies contribute to the preaching of the word, the administration of the sacraments, and the maintenance of pure teaching, they are justified."[2]

The church has therefore never developed organizational structures unique to itself but has borrowed them from the secular environment, adapting them as necessary. In chapter 5 we considered the research of Peter Rudge, who described the various organizational structures used by the church over the years.

- *Traditional:* The church is organized to maintain the tradition. Authority resides in the leader.
- *Charismatic:* The church has little organization, but follows the leader who pursues an intuition.
- *Classical:* The church is like a bureaucracy. The leaders "run the machine."
- *Human Relations:* The church is a network of groups. Leadership is leading groups.
- *Systems:* The church is like a body, a whole with many parts. Leadership clarifies purpose and interprets change.[3]

Peter Rudge believes that the systems view is most fitting for the church because of its close association with the body of Christ image of the church in the New Testament, and also because it results in a church that can more readily adapt to the changing circumstances and needs. Rudge states: "The systems way of thinking has the greatest weight of biblical support and is nearest to the central stream of Christian thinking."[4]

The systems view of organizational life sees the system as a whole and also three subsystems: input, transforming, and output.

The input system is made up of all of the resources that come together—the people and their various gifts, the money, the church staff, the influence of the environment. The transforming system is what happens to the raw material that comes through the input system—the people and their gifts, needs, and interests. The worship, classes, sacraments, fellowship, prayers—all are part of the transforming system. Some of it remains in the church and continues to influence the transforming system itself, but much of it moves the output system.

The output system is the means by which the church "exports" a part of its energy and resources (money, people, programs) in order to influence its environment or to support other organizations or causes. The members of the church who gather on Sunday morning and at other times are part of the input and transforming systems. After church, they scatter again, now as part of the output system where their calling is to be the salt of the earth and the light of the world. Meanwhile, a portion of the monetary gift that was given in church is distributed to various parts of the world through agencies and mission projects.

Organizing the church for its life and mission makes it possible for the church's resources to go toward the accomplishment of its goals.

STAFFING

If the church's plans and intentions are to be implemented, if the systems are to function and the life of the congregation is to be empowered, there must be a flow of talent to do the work and provide the necessary leadership and direction. This is the task of staffing—selecting, training, and developing people for the work of the church.

Staffing is therefore a broad function. In addition to the salaried church staff, it is appropriate to include as staff all who serve and lead in the church—those who teach classes and sing in choirs as well as those who serve on committees.

Much of what was considered in chapter 10 about team leadership is pertinent here. To supplement and give that broader application, consider insights on the subject from Douglas McGregor.[5]

McGregor identified and explained eight characteristics of well-functioning work groups or staffs.

173

1. *Understanding, mutual agreement, and identification with respect to the primary task* —clearly determining what business we are in.

This is properly at the head of the list, and is especially important for church workers where the appropriate model is not that of independent professionals or volunteers, but rather a team, functioning under the guidance of a common purpose in pursuit of common goals.

2. *Open communication* —meaning a genuine expression of ideas and feelings, of what some call "leveling."

The importance of this has already been emphasized. Here let it be noted that communication will usually happen only if provision is made for it. For example, the salaried staff of the church should have regular staff meetings. The members of the leadership and service groups must come together not only to do their business or service but to sustain communication, to convey information, to strengthen relationships.

3. *Mutual trust* —"I know that you will not—deliberately or accidentally, consciously or unconsciously—take unfair advantage of me."

This relationship, though somewhat idealistic for a large group, is nevertheless an appropriate goal and one that should be held before the group. It would enhance the life of any team of workers.

4. *Mutual support* —caring, concern, help, friendliness, love.

Again, this may seem idealistic. But remember, the idea here comes not from a church author or publisher, but from one who wrote for the business world. These characteristics would serve well in any and every setting.

5. *Management of human differences.* Differences do and will exist. Unless there are norms and rules to manage the differences, anarchy results and the team breaks down.

In chapter 13 we considered several different approaches to managing the conflict that inevitably arises when people work together, especially when they care deeply about what they are doing. The concluding section, "Handling Everyday Conflict Issues," will serve effectively for most of the conflict situations that arise, taking into consideration as well the varying affiliation, achievement, and power needs of people.

6. *Selective use of the team.* Not all managerial activity is appropriately carried out in a team setting. The team leader may confer with individuals and delegate particular activities.

This provision gives the staff leader the freedom to work with flexibility. He or she will decide when to bring a matter before the whole group, when to rely on individual consultation, and when to take independent action. Participatory leadership is the goal and the ideal, but sometimes the leader may take separate action.

7. *Appropriate member skills.* The combined results of the team should be such as to meet the requirements of the overall task.

Again, this applies not only to the salaried staff, which is obviously selected according to gifts, training, and skills, but to other leaders as well. Time and talent surveys, despite their shortcomings, are still beneficial. Nominating committees need to work with great deliberation, selecting candidates in light of the responsibilities of the position and the candidate's particular gifts. Also, because one of the basic assumptions of this book is that leaders are made, not born, it is important to provide everyone with training for their tasks.

8. *Leadership*—the personal qualifications, skills, role, and strategy of the team leader.

While care must be taken in the selection and placement of the entire staff, special care must be taken in selecting the group leader. He or she is the pacesetter, influencing not only the ambience and goals of the organization, but also how well those goals are achieved. For as McGregor states, it is well to consider not only the skills of the one to be chosen, but the personal qualifications as well. One may have the skills for the task, narrowly conceived, but may lack "people skills"—and therefore be unable to fulfill the responsibilities of the role.

Staffing involves the selection, training, and development of people who lead and serve in the church. Along with coordinating and organizing, staffing serves to build and edify the church for its life and mission.

While coordinating, organizing, and staffing are often viewed as the most mundane of the leadership tasks, they are essential to the life of any group, the church included. The church's mission is either enhanced or stymied, depending on how well these tasks are executed.

PART FIVE

FAITH ACTIVE
IN
LEADERSHIP

The wise leader models spiritual behavior and lives in harmony with spiritual values. There is a way of knowing, higher than reason; there is a self, greater than egocentricity.

John Heider

The Holy Spirit is not the missing link in our management techniques and action plans. He is the enabling power of Christ himself working with and through our struggles to do what is right as well as what is effective, so that in the end, Christ is glorified.

Ray S. Anderson

15

LEADERSHIP AND SPIRITUALITY

Toward the end of his Gospel, John recorded a conversation between Peter and the risen Christ that has to do with both the care and leadership of the church:

> When they had finished breakfast, Jesus said to Simon Peter, "Simon, son of John, do you love me more than these?" He said to him, "Yes, Lord, you know that I love you." He said to him, "Feed my lambs." A second time he said to him, "Simon, son of John, do you love me?" He said to him, "Yes, Lord, you know that I love you." He said to him, "Tend my sheep." He said to him a third time, "Simon, son of John, do you love me?" . . . And he said to him, "Lord, you know everything; you know that I love you." Jesus said to him, "Feed my sheep."
>
> (John 21:15–17)

Love for Christ is fundamental and indispensable for the care and leadership of Christ's people. Three times the question was

179

asked: "Do you love me?" And when Peter responded in the affirmative, he was told to feed and tend the flock.

Feeding God's people has to do with word and sacrament, with reading and preaching the Scriptures and with breaking the bread in Communion. It is nourishing God's people in the life of faith and devotion.

To tend the flock is not the same as to feed it. While the Greek word for feeding is *boskein*, the word for tend is *poimainein*— words with different meanings. Raymond Brown writes, "Those who feed (*boskein*) supply nourishment, but those who tend (*poimainein*) have the power of rulers and governors."[1] The people of God need not only nourishment from the Word and sacrament; they need as well the nourishment that comes from the right quality and quantity of leadership and organizational attention.

In this chapter we consider the relationship between the responsibilities of leadership and the spiritual aspects of life and faith.

To some, there is no relationship, except perhaps as opposites. A flyer in the mail advertising a workshop on leadership for church workers reflected this view when it asked, "Are You a Spiritual Leader?" It went on to distinguish spiritual leaders from secular leaders by pointing out that spiritual leaders focus primarily on building and nurturing people, while secular leaders focus primarily on building organizations; that spiritual leaders focus on helping people grow, while secular leaders focus on organizing people to get jobs done; that spiritual leaders are concerned with motivating toward discipleship, while secular leaders are concerned with controlling behavior. To those who planned the workshop and prepared the flyer, there was apparently no relationship between spirituality and organizational life.

The approach in this book is quite different. It has been to distinguish the spiritual from the secular, and then to integrate them in responsible ways. Taking our clue from the incarnation of Christ, it seems entirely fitting to assume that we serve Christ in and through the organizational life of the church, expressing our spirituality in the process.

When reading secular literature on the subject of leadership, I frequently come across statements that remind me that leadership is more than organizing, controlling, and getting jobs done. There is another dimension to leadership. Whether in secular organizations or the church, leadership has a spiritual dimension.

WHAT SECULAR AUTHORS ARE SAYING

Harlan Cleveland, former dean of the Humphrey Institute of Public Affairs at the University of Minnesota, talks about the importance of the leader's attitude, which is more important, he says, than skill. In a summary of the essence of leadership, Cleveland cites these as the primary ingredients: intellectual curiosity, genuine interest in people, a willingness to risk, an awareness that crises are normal, and a feeling of responsibility for envisioning the future as well as for the general outcome of the leader's efforts.[2] Cleveland's insights suggest a spiritual dimension to leadership awareness and practice.

Military leader General Edward C. Meyer writes about the importance of knowledge in the leadership role, and of the ability to apply that knowledge to the specific needs of the hour. But character is the basic quality of the leader, says Meyer—character embodied in one who has high ideals, who stands by them, and who can be trusted absolutely. In Meyer's words, "Character is an ingrained principle expressed consciously and unconsciously to subordinates, superiors and peers alike—honesty, loyalty, courage, self-confidence, humility and self-sacrifice. Its expression to all audiences must ring with authenticity."[3]

John Clemens and Douglas Mayer, the authors of *The Classic Touch*, are in accord with this when they say that we live in a world in which hunch, intuition, self-assurance, and openness to new ideas are more important to success than technical skills.

What separates great business leaders from the not-so-great often has more to do with what we call "the classic touch"—the artistry of getting others to commit themselves to their highest possible levels of achievement—than with specialized techniques. Knowledge of finance, marketing, production, and personnel is important, of course; but it often produces the kind of leader who, although able to name every single tree, may fail to notice that the forest is burning. What is needed is a broader view of leadership grounded in literature that focuses, not on specialized techniques, but rather on the vast human side of the leadership equation.[4]

This results in what James MacGregor Burns called "transforming leadership"—leadership that is "morally purposeful" and elevating. "The transforming leader taps the needs and raises the aspirations and helps shape the values—and hence mobilizes the potential—of followers."[5] Burns concludes his book with this sentence: "That people can be lifted into their better selves is the secret of transforming leadership and the moral and practical theme of this work."[6]

Warren Bennis and Burt Nanus make a distinction between leaders and managers by saying that leaders operate on the emotional and spiritual resources of the organization, the values, commitments, and aspirations, while managers operate on the physical resources, the capital, the human skills, the technology. They write:

> Great leaders often inspire their followers to high levels of achievement by showing them how their work contributes to worthwhile ends. It is an emotional appeal to some of the most fundamental of human needs—the need to be important, to make a difference, to be a part of a worthwhile and successful enterprise.[7]

Psychologist John Heider is more specific and more in accord with the Christian faith when he states that wise leaders will model spiritual behavior and live in harmony with spiritual values, demonstrating the power of selflessness and the unity of all creation. He writes: "Be willing to speak of traditional religion, no matter how offended some group members may be. Overcome the bias against the word 'God.' The great force of our spiritual roots lies in tradition, like it or not."[8]

Michael Maccoby in *The Leader* also appeals for attention to the spiritual dimension of life, arguing that it is the true basis of integrity:

> The study of the Bible, comparative religion, ethical philosophy and psychology, and great literature leads one to explore the inner life,

particularly the struggle to develop the human heart against igno-
rance, convention, injustice, disappointment, betrayal, and irra-
tional passion. Such an education prepares one to grapple with his
fear, envy, pride, and self-deception. It raises questions about the
nature of human destructiveness and the legitimate use of force.
Without it, a would-be leader tends to confuse his or her own character with human nature, guts with courage, worldly success with
integrity, the thrill of winning with happiness.[9]

Maccoby goes on to encourage the "drum major instinct" of
Martin Luther King, Jr., nurtured by reading the Bible, the philosophy of ethics, literature, and psychology that probes the human spirit. All of these, he believes, will develop and strengthen
leadership in our time.

SPIRITUAL REALITIES AND ORGANIZATIONAL PRINCIPLES

What about the insights that are unique to the Christian faith
and the spirituality that comes of it? In his book *Wheel Within the
Wheel*, Richard Hutcheson both criticizes and appreciates the
church's use of secular leadership and management techniques.
He would not have us uncritically use them, but neither would he
have us reject them as being useless or inappropriate for the life of
the church. "The Holy Spirit is the church's most basic organizational principle," writes Hutcheson. "Everything that enhances
this trust and enables the Spirit thus to work through the church
is valid."[10]

Hutcheson describes what he believes are the organizational
implications of the church's most characteristic activities.[11]

Prayer. In organizational terms, prayer is a form of communication within the community as well as with the Lord, and also a
form of empowerment that can be brought to bear on any and all
aspects of organizational life. It is also, says Hutcheson, a means of
expressing the unity of the organization.

Confession and Forgiveness. In organizational terms confession
is acknowledgment of the fallibility of the organization as well

as the individuals within it. Through the promise of forgiveness there is the hope of renewal and change, which strengthens the interpersonal relationships and the organization as a whole.

Worship. "It is the primary way of developing, expressing and experiencing the unity of the organization in its achievement of its purposes and pursuit of its goals."[12] Worship, says Hutcheson, recognizes the authority basis of the organization and is a way of maintaining organizational health.

Use of Scripture. As with prayer, the use of Scripture is a communication process. Now, however, the direction is changed, coming from God to the church. The written Word, says Hutcheson, is the official record of the early stages of the organization and is the source of the organization's continuing guidance.

Sacraments. They, too, are a form of communication. Ceremonial activities with symbolic significance, the sacraments are also a form of participation by members in the organizational life, offering a corporate experience of the Holy Spirit.

Preaching. This, says Hutcheson, is an extremely important expression of internal communication, as well as communication from the Lord. It also serves as one of the organization's key motivational activities.

Hutcheson's purpose in this is to show that the church's characteristic activities, derived from its transcendent dimension, are applicable to the church's organizational life and needs. He writes: "To look at their organizational implications is not to debase them or the spiritual dimension of the church. It is, rather, to bring the organizational dimension into congruence with the spiritual dimension of the church."[13]

LEADERSHIP AND VISION

In chapter 11 we discussed the importance of vision for an organization and its leaders, highlighting the significance of this for the church. The vision for the church does not spring from the leader's mind or from out of the blue, but from reading the Scriptures and from reflection on the contemporary needs of the church, the community, and the larger world.

Theologian Ray Anderson further develops this concept when he states that the church's vision is developed not from the present to the future, but from the future to the present. This, he says, is because in the church we live first by the promises of God—"the one who sees the sign of God's promise is first of all a student of the promises!"[14] Second, says Anderson, we are to be students of the times, taking our cue from Karl Barth, who studied and reflected on the Bible in one hand and the daily newspaper in the other. There is nothing esoteric about the Christian vision, nor is it something achievable only by persons with a mystical quality. Rather, says Anderson, "It is a gift one can develop through meditation on God's revealed Word and serious attention to the human situation and the historical present."[15]

LEADERSHIP AND FAITH, HOPE, AND LOVE

The Christian virtues of faith, hope, and love have close parallels in the exercise of leadership.

Faith may be associated with vision, and gives birth to the vision. We refer here to faith in the promises of God for the world and the church. These promises, fulfilled in and through Christ, take historical form and shape when the church faithfully pursues goals that are in accord with the promises. Faith is therefore necessary for church leaders. Without faith and a vision that is shaped by the promises of God and a careful discernment of the times, church leaders are the blind leading the blind.

Hope may be associated with confidence, countering the despair and discouragement that are never far away. Hope, like faith, is rooted in the promises of God and in the vision that comes of those promises, viewed in the context of our time. Hope thus flows back into the present, empowering the people of hope for continuing ministry and service, encouraging them even when there is little reason for encouragement. People of hope live with the confidence that God will fulfill God's promises.

Love may be associated with motivation, and is its most basic power. Jesus' question of Peter cited at the beginning of the chapter asked, "Simon Peter, son of John, do you love me?" Apparently Jesus knew that unless Peter's heart was right, his words to Peter would be in vain. The tending and feeding would be too strenuous. Apart from the deepest of motives—the profound affection and commitment of the heart—there would be no lasting mission. The question Christ asked Peter is asked of all who would lead in the church: "Do you love me?"

Faith, hope, and love—these three abide: in our interpersonal relationships, in our congregational life, and in fulfilling our leadership responsibilities. The church helps sustain faith, hope, and love. The church, in turn, is enriched when faith, hope, and love are expressed throughout its life. As leaders we do not separate our spiritual lives from our leadership responsibilities. Rather, we seek their integration, for we serve Christ when we lead as well as when we worship and pray.

16

THE LEADER'S PERSONAL LIFE

Leadership can be hazardous to your health. To be a leader is to bear the burden of responsibility, endure tension, face criticism. Some surrender the leadership role because of its weight, some burn out under its demands.

In this chapter we consider the leader's personal life in order to help leaders endure the responsibilities and lead with vision, perseverance, and joy.

Our lives may well be "hid with Christ in God," but they are still subject to God's laws of nature. And they are still terminal. We must give them the attention and care they need.

THE BODY FACTOR

Yes, hear it one more time—take care of your body. Eat right. Exercise. Get enough rest. Our spiritual growth, as well as effectiveness in other areas of life, including that of leadership—it often depends on what we do with our bodies.

Herbert Chilstrom, bishop of the Evangelical Lutheran Church in America, writes about this in an article addressed to pastors. He states, "I am convinced, on the basis of both my own experience, as well as that of pastors with whom I counsel, that many pastors are so neglectful of the care of their bodies that they cannot possibly fulfill the demands of their calling."[1] Chilstrom advocates a five-part program that a midwestern corporation devised for its employees:

1. If you smoke, quit.
2. If you use alcohol at all, let it be with strict moderation.
3. Begin some regimen of physical exercise; a minimum of fifteen minutes a day for at least five days each week.
4. Keep within ten pounds of your ideal weight.
5. Get an average of seven hours of sleep daily.

Chilstrom cites E. Stanley Jones as an example of one who neglected his body until he was in his early 40s. Prompted by periods of ill health and exhaustion, he dedicated himself to a new way of living, respecting his body's need for rest, exercise, and proper diet. As a result, Jones discovered new resources of energy and he maintained a vigorous life until he was well into his 80s. So, leaders, take care of your body. Remember, it is the temple of the Holy Spirit!

THE TIME FACTOR

If Parkinson's Law is true—work expands to fill the time available for its completion—it is because we allow it to be true. Work does not in fact expand, but we may allow distractions and daydreams to deplete the time that could otherwise be used to complete it. Because leaders have much to do, they ought to make the best use of their time.

Any bookstore will have one or more volumes on time management, and what they say can be helpful. But what needs to be said on the subject can be said more briefly. Here is a short list of time-management ideas:

1. Get up and get going in the morning.
2. Get organized.
   —Plan your work.
   —Follow a daily To Do list.
   —Exercise self-discipline.

3. Avoid time wasters.
   —Procrastination.
   —Overinvolvement in details.
   —Confused priorities.
   —Perfectionist tendencies.
4. Get to bed on time.

The Bible talks about time in two ways—as *chronos*, meaning chronological time; and as *kairos*, meaning time of opportunity. The time factor under discussion has to do mainly with *chronos*, with ways of making the best use of the gift of time that is marked by minutes, hours, days, and years. But the concern is for *kairos* as well. For unless we manage the gift of *chronos*, we may miss the gift of *kairos*—and the opportunities God sets before us.

THE CENTERING AND PRAYER FACTORS

Church leaders ought to pray, and ought to make their leadership responsibilities the subject of their prayers. Consider these reasons:

First, pray to truly come under the lordship of Christ. This is the primary Christian perspective. We may commit ourselves to political views of one kind or another, to different philosophies and outlooks, to various theories of leadership, but our primary commitment is to Jesus Christ. "Hold fast to Christ," said historian Herbert Butterfield, "but for the rest remain totally uncommitted."[2]

Second, pray to see your entire life as an expression of the faith. This is our primary calling—to live out our confession of faith in all that we do. But it does not come naturally; it is the result of discipline and perseverance, of careful thought and intentional prayer.

Third, pray to counter the creeping dangers of power and pride—special dangers, it seems, for people in leadership positions. While both power and pride have the potential for good—the power resulting in change for the better, and the pride resulting in a more positive self-image—there are negative possibilities as well. We must scrutinize our intentions, our plans, our actions in the context of prayer and self-examination.

Fourth, pray to empower yourself for the price of leadership. Those with little leadership experience seem unaware of the price to be paid. They see only status, recognition, honor. But there is another side to the experience—sacrifice, criticism, fatigue, loneliness, long hours. As a result, some burn out and give up and some steer clear of the burdens of leadership. Others, however, accept the challenge and stand ready to pay the price. To pray is to be empowered for the task.

Fifth, pray to keep hope alive. Christians live in the context of God's promised future. Although our faith is rooted in the events of the past, we appropriately turn toward the future, anticipating the new heaven and the new earth, the day when "death shall be no more" and when "the former things have passed away" (Revelation 21). Through centering, Scripture reading, meditation, and prayer, hope is kept alive and we are empowered to live in accord with the apostle's prayer: "May the God of hope fill you with all joy and peace in believing, so that by the power of the Holy Spirit you may abound in hope" (Rom. 15:13).

METHODS AND MATERIALS

What should leaders read and how should they pray? While the supply of literature is vast, we identify a short list of resources that may be helpful to those with leadership responsibilities.

Key Scripture Passages

Psalm 46. Not only does this reading remind us that God is our "refuge and strength"—it reminds us that God is the Lord of all, before whom we are to "be still."

Psalm 103. The Lord is the one "who forgives all your iniquity, who heals all your diseases" and while "our days are like grass," they are lived out in God's presence.

Mark 10:35–45. James and John wanted the seats of honor in the coming kingdom. Their request led to this significant passage about the meaning of discipleship and the shape of Christian leadership.

Romans 12:1–13. This passage tells us that God gives a variety of gifts to the church, all of which are to be generously used for the well-being of the whole church. See also 1 Corinthians 12.

Hebrews 10:23–25. This reading recognizes that God's gifts may be allowed to languish unused. We are urged to "stir up one another to love and good works."

1 Peter 4:9–11. Peter encourages his readers to practice hospitality, to be gracious and genuine in relationship to others. Is this true especially for leaders?

1 Thessalonians 2:4. This is a short passage, just one verse, but it speaks of something essential for leaders, namely, accountability. Whom do we please in our practice of leadership? What does it mean to please God?

1 Timothy 3:8–13. Here Paul describes some of the qualities of church leaders. They must not be "greedy for gain" but serious and faithful.

MEDITATION AND PRAYER

M. Basil Pennington, author of *Centering Prayer*, suggests taking three deep breaths at the beginning of your meditation and prayer time. He recommends the following: First, get settled comfortably in a straight-back chair. Second, gently close your eyes. Third, allow the air in your lungs to seep out, not forcing it. Fourth, inhale deeply, hold your breath for a few moments, then release it, allowing the air to flow out again. Repeat this step two more times, and then turn your attention to the Presence.[3]

Consider the statement by John Westerhoff and John Eusden, which emphasizes the importance of prayer and meditation:

> For too long we have thought of the Christian life as essentially either involvement in political, economic, social concerns that wear us out and result in depression or activity which keeps the church intact and doctrinally pure. Our primary orientation cannot be an institution or some great cause or even other people, but first and forever to God. Unless our identity is hid in God we will never know who we are or what we are to do. Our first act must be prayer. To be human is to pray, to meditate both day and night on the love and activity of God. We are called to be continuously

formed and transformed by the thought of God within us. Prayer is a disciplined dedication to paying attention. Without the single-minded attention of prayer we will rarely hear anything worth repeating or catch a vision worth asking anyone else to gaze upon.[4]

Howard Thurman's prayer "I Need Thy Sense of Order" has special appeal to leaders caught in the disarray of conflicting demands and expectations:

> The confusion of the details of living
> Is sometimes overwhelming. The little things
> Keep getting in my way providing ready-made
> Excuses for failure to do and be
> What I know I ought to know and be.
> Much time is spent on things that are not very
>   important
> While significant things are put into an insignificant
>   place
> In my scheme of order. I must unscramble my affairs
> So that my life will become order. O God, I need
>   thy sense of order.[5]

Our meditation and prayers will focus on God and renew our relationship to him, but they will also connect with the issues of our everyday lives. For leaders, meditation and prayer will frequently center on decisions to make, problems to face, plans to develop. Often they will center on the persons we lead, their needs and situation. Lloyd Ogilvie lists a series of questions for leaders to consider in their time of meditation.

- Do we love the people we lead?
- Do they know it?
- Do they know that we will their ultimate good?
- Do they share in formulating the direction we give?
- Have we helped them set reasonable goals?
- Do we stand with them in costly involvement?
- Are we vulnerable enough to admit our own failures so that the ambience of grace is communicated?[6]

Ogilvie recognizes that leaders are also followers, so he has a second list of questions prompting thought about those who lead us.

- Do we pray for the people who lead us?
- Do we communicate our support for our leaders?
- Are we willing to participate in the setting of direction?
- Are we willing to support a decision once it is made and not saw sawdust?
- Do we give our leaders the freedom to fail and the grace to begin again?[7]

Martin Luther's Prayers

Luther's Morning Prayer has been used by countless numbers: In the morning when you arise, say: "In the name of the Father, and of the Son, and of the Holy Spirit. Amen." Then, kneeling or standing, say the Apostles' Creed and the Lord's Prayer. Then say this prayer:

I give you thanks, heavenly Father, through Jesus Christ your dear Son, that you have protected me through the night from all danger and harm; and I pray that you will preserve and keep me this day also from all sin and evil; that in all my thoughts, words, and deeds, I may serve and please you. Into your hands I commend my body and soul, and all that is mine. Let your holy angel have charge concerning me that the wicked one have no power over me. Amen.

After a hymn, or the Ten Commandments, or whatever your devotion may suggest, you should go with joy to your work.

Luther's Evening Prayer has also stood the test of time: In the evening when you go to bed, say this: "In the name of the Father, and of the Son, and of the Holy Spirit. Amen." Then, kneeling or standing, say the Apostles' Creed and the Lord's Prayer. Then you may say this prayer:

I give thanks to you, heavenly Father, through Jesus Christ, your dear Son, that you have this day so graciously protected me, and I pray that you will forgive me all my sins and the wrongs which

I have done, and by your great mercy defend me from all the perils and dangers of this night. Into your hands I commend my body and soul, and all that is mine. Let your holy angel have charge concerning me, that the wicked one have no power over me. Amen.

Lie down in peace and sleep.[8]

St. Ignatius's Evening Devotions

Those who prefer something less formal than Luther's Evening Prayer, and yet want an order to follow, may find the five-step format of St. Ignatius of Loyola helpful.

- *Thanksgiving*
  Review the day's events and blessings.
- *Illumination*
  See yourself as a child of God in need of healing.
- *Assessment*
  Take inventory of the day, using Jesus as your model.
- *Forgiveness*
  Remember that Jesus came not to condemn but to redeem and to save.
- *Pray for Renewal*
  Ask God—Father, Son, and Holy Spirit—to be present and to give you peace and power.

KEEPING THE LILT IN LIFE

Leaders often get weighed down with concerns, anxieties, and a sense of futility. Such attitudes and feelings are to be resisted and overcome. While a degree of vulnerability is appropriate—leaders *are* human—they are leaders in attitude and in spirit, as well as in action and behavior. Leaders set the tone of an organization. For the good of the organization, it is important that its leaders keep the lilt in life.

Fred Smith, a businessman who speaks to church groups, writes about this in his book *You and Your Network*. He speaks of the power of wonderment, urgency, reverence, and gratitude to aerate life, helping to maintain the lilt in life.

Wonderment, says Smith, is the sense of awe that comes from merely opening your eyes to the world around us. Urgency comes from having something important to believe and do. Reverence is due God, says Smith, but reverence is also due God's creation; and gratitude is the healthiest of all emotions. To keep the lilt in life, encourage and provide for wonderment, urgency, reverence, and gratitude. You will be a happier person and a more effective leader.[9]

A PRAYER FOR ALL SEASONS

The *Service of Matins* in the Lutheran Book of Worship includes a prayer that could be called a prayer for all seasons, one that is fitting for both leaders and followers, and under circumstances of all kinds.

Lord God, you have called your servants to ventures of which we cannot see the ending, by paths as yet untrodden, through perils unknown. Give us faith to go out with good courage, not knowing where we go, but only that your hand is leading us and your love supporting us; through Jesus Christ our Lord.

Leaders are public people, often in the public eye. As such they are subject to temptations of arrogance and undue pride, susceptible to the inroads of cynicism and burnout, fatigue and the loss of courage and resolve. To be effective, leaders must give attention to their own lives, to care for their bodies, as well as their souls— to eat, exercise, and rest, as well as to pray, meditate, and worship.

AFTERWORD

Before bringing this sampler on leadership to a close, it seems appropriate to glance back, noting once again some of the highlights of our study, and a glance forward, to suggest possibilities for leadership development in the future.

Amid all the quotations and references, what are the key insights? What do I want to point to as the basic and most important affirmations? And what about leadership development in the days ahead?

First, the practice of leadership in the church is rooted in the faith of the church. From the perspective of the biblical record, leadership is a gift, a calling, and a ministry.

As a gift of God to the church, leadership is given for the church's welfare and well-being, and for the sake of its ministry and mission. While leadership may seem to be nothing more than a utilitarian function—after all, leadership is necessary—the biblical record says it is also a gift of God's Spirit to the church.

As a calling, the leadership role is a means of fulfilling one's vocation, and is a calling to a position, a relationship, or, more

197

likely, to a series of relationships, and to responsibilities that are expressed through specific actions.

As a ministry, leadership is a way in which God's people are served to equip them for their own ministry or to guide the church in faithfulness to the cause of Christ.

Second, the basic style for leaders in the church is that of a servant. Taking our clue from the Lord of the church who came "not to be served but to serve," we lead by serving and we serve by leading.

In the Bible there are many different expressions of leadership. There we find Moses the visionary, Joshua the strategic planner, Paul the communicator. But all were servants, all served God and God's people.

Robert Greenleaf has emphasized this in a special way through the development of the servant-leader concept. Too often, he says, church leaders settle for the maintenance aspects of leadership—managing and administering. As necessary as these activities are, the result is neither a well-served church nor society. Leadership is also initiating, says Greenleaf—going out ahead to show the way. And this, he maintains, is the way church leaders serve. They serve by leading and they lead by serving.

Third, pastors have unique leadership responsibilities, and can properly see themselves as pastoral leaders. For too long pastors have labored under an unduly narrow understanding of what it means to be a servant. Our image of a servant comes more from the role of a server in a fast-food restaurant, I'm afraid, than from the Scripture or the example of Jesus. The server in the restaurant does what the customer wants, is subservient to the wishes of the customer, serves the desires and felt needs of the customer.

Jesus did not limit his leadership in such a way. While he obviously came to serve, he usually determined the shape and expression of the service himself. He served the deeper needs of people, needs that were often not even recognized. He was a servant leader. He expressed the mind and will of the Father; he saw the deeper needs of people and he sought to serve those deeper needs.

The pastor, as servant-leader, takes cues from that image. He or she does not ignore or run roughshod over the expressed needs of people. But the pastor has the unique opportunity to lead the people to awareness of deeper needs, and to the awareness of God's will and way for human life and society. The servant-leader image described by Robert Greenleaf was profoundly expressed by Jesus of Nazareth and deserves to be the model for pastors of the church.

Greenleaf's critique of our society and its leaders applies as well to the church:

> Who is the enemy? Who is holding back more rapid movement to the better society that is reasonable and possible with available resources? Who is responsible for the mediocre performance of so many of our institutions? Who is standing in the way of a larger consensus on the definition of the better society and paths to reach it? Not evil people. Not stupid people. Not apathetic people. Not the "system." . . . The real enemy is fuzzy thinking on the part of good, intelligent, vital people, and their failure to lead, and to follow servants as leaders.[1]

Pastors need not be mere maintainers of churches. They are pastoral leaders, to use the image set forth in chapter 8, who serve by leading and who lead by serving.

Fourth, church leaders do more than maintain the status quo. Nor are they merely "transactional" leaders as described by James MacGregor Burns—swapping one thing for another, overseeing the events that take place. Church leaders are what Burns calls "transforming" leaders—leaders who seek to satisfy the higher needs of people, whose leadership raises the level of human conduct and aspiration, transforming leader and follower as well as the existing situation.

While Burns does not draw his insights directly from biblical religion, the harmony between his position and that which is expressed in the Bible is obvious. The Old Testament prophets, for example, calling for repentance and faith, for a new direction in life, motivated not by greed but by the command of God, were transforming leaders of the first order. So, too, were Jesus, John the

Baptist, and the apostles. Indeed, Christ's great commission to the church—to make disciples of all nations—was a commission to be a transforming leader in the world at large.

Church leaders, called to be the salt of the earth and the light of the world, are therefore transforming leaders.

Fifth, leaders are usually not born, as is sometimes said; leaders are more often made, and are the products of learning and experience, of insights, coaching, and practice. While leaders were at one time born to both rank and wealth, now they are mostly made through education, modeling, and practice.

This does not mean, however, that there are no identifiable leadership qualities. As indicated in chapter 7, the research of Warren Bennis and Burt Nanus discovered four common traits among effective leaders: commitment to a vision, effective communication skills, reliability, and self-awareness. Complementing this is Harlan Cleveland's description of leaders:

> They are strategic thinkers, more inclined than their followers to relate things and people to each other, to project patterns of collective behavior, to keep trying to see the situation whole. They are unusually curious about issues and methods outside the specialties in which they got their start. They are more preoccupied with values and purposes than their contemporaries and former fellow specialists; that is, they are more likely to cut through the forest of how-to questions and ask "Why?" They are the optimists, the visionaries—the people who, confronted by the gloom and reluctance that are the hallmarks of expertise, are more inclined to ask, "Why not?" And they are the folk who actually seem to enjoy the complexity of it all.[2]

How do leaders obtain such qualities? Not usually through birth, but through their entire life's experience—often through the intentional effort to gain the understanding and skills that leadership roles require. If leadership is a gift of the Spirit, it is nevertheless a gift that can be informed, nourished, and practiced. If it is a talent, it is a talent that can be strengthened and improved. Leadership principles can be conceptualized and learned; leadership skills can be improved; leadership practices can be enlightened. Leaders are not born; leaders are made.

Three significant needs in today's church—to clarify the vision, to communicate it, and to motivate people's response—can all be met by the right kind and quality of leadership, leadership that is adequately informed and intelligently practiced.

In addition to reading such books as are listed in For Further Study, and the variety of workshops that are available under the auspices of theological seminaries, some universities and colleges also offer programs in leadership education. For example:

- Augsburg College, Minneapolis, Minnesota, offers a Master of Arts in Leadership within the context of a liberal arts curriculum.
- Colorado College combines a series of visiting lecturers with community service activities.
- Duke University has a program that combines liberal arts classroom components with community projects.
- Princeton University provides a program of lectures by effective leaders.
- Stanford University has a program that is rooted in literature.
- As this book is being completed a church leadership institute is being developed in the Twin Cities of Minneapolis and St. Paul, Minnesota.

Leadership is a gift, calling, and ministry that is always in a state of development. We learn from our own experience, and we learn from others. Leadership deserves continuing development, for it is often the means through which God's purposes are fulfilled, in both the church and world at large.

NOTES

PREFACE

1. James MacGregor Burns, *Leadership* (New York: Harper & Row, 1978), 2.
2. Warren Bennis and Burt Nanus, *Leaders: The Strategies for Taking Charge* (New York: Harper & Row, 1985), 4.
3. Ralph M. Stogdill, *Handbook of Leadership* (New York: Free Press, 1974), 580.
4. Paul Tillich, *Systematic Theology* (Chicago: University of Chicago Press, 1963), 3:81–82.
5. Burns, *Leadership*, 1–2.
6. Edward Schillebeeckx, *Ministry: Leadership in the Community of Jesus Christ* (New York: Crossroad, 1984), 1.
7. Kennon Callahan, *Twelve Keys to an Effective Church* (San Francisco: Harper & Row, 1983), 41.

CHAPTER 1: A GIFT, A CALLING, A MINISTRY

1. Edward Schillebeeckx, *Ministry: Leadership in the Community of Jesus Christ* (New York: Crossroad, 1984), 15.
2. The Constitution of the Evangelical Lutheran Church in America, chap. 5, para. h.
3. Quoted by Martin E. Marty in *Context* 18 (December 15, 1986):3–4.
4. Quoted by Rueben P. Job and Norman Shawchuck, *A Guide to Prayer for Ministers and Other Servants* (Nashville: Upper Room), 68.

CHAPTER 2: FOR WHAT PURPOSE?

1. Quoted by Warren Bennis and Burt Nanus, *Leaders: The Strategies for Taking Charge* (New York: Harper & Row, 1985), 22.
2. Ibid.

3. John W. Gardner, *The Tasks of Leadership* (Washington: Independent Sector, 1986), 7.
4. Ibid., 20.
5. Robert K. Greenleaf, *Servant Leadership* (New York: Paulist Press, 1977), 80.
6. James MacGregor Burns, *Leadership* (New York: Harper & Row, 1978), 4.
7. Ibid., 19.
8. Greenleaf, *Servant Leadership*, 49.
9. Ibid., 146–47.
10. Ibid., 80.
11. Ibid., 81.
12. Ibid., 82.

CHAPTER 3: THE MAKING OF LEADERS

1. Martin M. Chemers, "The Social, Organizational, and Cultural Context of Effective Leadership," in *Leadership: Multidisciplinary Perspectives*, ed. Barbara Kellerman (Englewood Cliffs, N.J.: Prentice-Hall, 1984), 38–39.
2. Edward Wynne, "What About Teaching Leadership?" in *AGB Reports* 26 (March/April 1984):38–39. Association of Governing Boards of Universities and Colleges, Washington, D.C.
3. Janet O. Hagberg, *Real Power* (Minneapolis: Winston Press, 1984), 1–148.
4. Ibid., 45.
5. Ibid., 73.
6. Ibid., 153.
7. Robert R. Blake and Jane Srygley Mouton, *The Managerial Grid III: The Key to Leadership Excellence* (Houston: Gulf Publishing, 1985), 12. Copyright © 1985; reproduced by permission.
8. Adapted from *Applied Management Newsletter* 8 (May 1985):1; National Association of Management, Wichita, Kansas.
9. Lyle E. Schaller, *The Decision Makers* (Nashville: Abingdon Press, 1974), 177.
10. Robert Tannebaum and Warren Schmidt, "How to Choose a Leadership Pattern," *Harvard Business Review* (May-June 1973). Reprinted by permission of Harvard Business Review. Copyright © 1973 by the President and Fellows of Harvard College; all rights reserved.

11. Quoted in John K. Clemens and Douglas F. Mayer, *The Classic Touch* (Homewood: Dow Jones-Irwin, 1987), 155.
12. Paul Hersey, *The Situational Leader* (New York: Warner Books, 1984), 43. Copyrighted material from Leadership Studies, Inc. All rights reserved. Used by permission.
13. Ibid., 68.
14. Kenneth Blanchard, *Leadership and the One Minute Manager* (New York: William Morrow, 1986), 68.
15. Ibid., 57.
16. Lyle E. Schaller, *Getting Things Done* (Nashville: Abingdon Press, 1986), 107.
17. Ibid.
18. Ibid.
19. Ibid., 107-9.

CHAPTER 4: LEADER: KNOW YOURSELF
1. Douglas McGregor, *The Human Side of Enterprise* (New York: McGraw-Hill, 1960), 182.
2. Michael Maccoby, *The Leader* (New York: Simon & Schuster, 1981), 61.
3. Edwin H. Friedman, *Generation to Generation* (New York: Guilford Press, 1985), 221.
4. Maccoby, *Leader*, 61.
5. Joseph Luft, *Group Processes*, 3d ed. (Palo Alto: Mayfield Publishing Co., 1984), 60.
6. Sherod Miller, Elam W. Nunnally, and Daniel B. Wackman, *Couple Communication I: Talking Together* (Minneapolis: Interpersonal Communication Programs, 1979), 161. For more information see *Connecting with Self and Others* by Miller et al. Call 1-800-328-5099.
7. David Keirsey and Marilyn Bates, *Please Understand Me* (Del Mar, CA.: Gnosology Books, 1984), 133-34.
8. Ibid., 139.
9. Ibid., 144.
10. Ibid., 148-49.
11. Friedman, *Generation to Generation*, 221.

CHAPTER 5: KNOWING YOUR ORGANIZATION
1. H. Richard Niebuhr, *The Purpose of the Church and Its Ministry* (New York: Harper & Row, 1956), 19-27.

2. "Apology to the Augsburg Confession," in *The Book of Concord*, trans. and ed. Theodore G. Tappert (Philadelphia: Muhlenberg Press, 1959), 169.
3. Ibid.
4. The Constitution of the Evangelical Lutheran Church in America, chap. 4, paras. 4.01; 4.03.
5. Philip Yancey, "The Church as Platypus," *Leadership* 7 (Summer 1986): 104–14.
6. Ibid., 105.
7. Ibid., 110.
8. Ibid., 111.
9. Richard G. Hutcheson, Jr., *Wheel Within the Wheel* (Atlanta: John Knox Press, 1979), 101–2.
10. Ibid., 104.
11. Ibid., 105.
12. Peter F. Rudge, *Ministry and Management* (London: Tavistock Publications, 1968), 66.
13. Ibid., 53.
14. Ibid.
15. See Alvin J. Lindgren and Norman Shawchuck, *Management for Your Church* (Nashville: Abingdon Press, 1977); James D. Anderson, *To Come Alive!* (New York: Harper & Row, 1973); and Robert C. Worley, *Change in the Church: A Source of Hope* (Philadelphia: Westminster Press, 1971).
16. Lindgren and Shawchuck, *Management for Your Church*, 24.

CHAPTER 6: KNOWING POWER AND AUTHORITY

1. James MacGregor Burns, *Leadership* (New York: Harper & Row, 1978), 9.
2. Ibid., 372.
3. David C. McClelland and David H. Burnham, "Power is the Great Motivator," *Harvard Business Review* 54 (March-April, 1976): 100–106.
4. John W. Gardner, *The Nature of Leadership* (Washington: Independent Sector, 1986), 7.
5. Rollo May, *Power and Innocence: A Search for the Sources of Violence* (New York: W. W. Norton, 1972), 105–11.
6. Quoted in ibid., 111.
7. Ibid., 113.

8. James H. Craig and Marguerite Craig, *Synergic Power* (Berkeley: Proactive Press, 1979), 64.
9. Robert C. Worley, *A Gathering of Strangers* (Philadelphia: Westminster Press, 1976), 31.
10. Ibid.
11. Burns, *Leadership*, 11.
12. Ibid.
13. Ibid., 15.
14. Michael Maccoby, *The Leader* (New York: Simon & Schuster, 1981), 223.
15. Anne Wilson Schaef, *Women's Reality* (Minneapolis: Winston Press, 1981), 125.
16. Ibid., 125–26.
17. Roy M. Oswald and Joan B. Bowman, *Women and Men Together* (Washington: Alban Institute, 1983), 30.
18. Robert Terry, *Leadership: Definitions, Dimensions, Directions* (Minneapolis: University Media Resources, 1986), 22.
19. Ibid., 23.
20. Richard J. Foster, *Money, Sex & Power* (San Francisco: Harper & Row, 1985), 207–11.

CHAPTER 7: QUALITIES OF LEADERS

1. Warren Bennis, "Four Traits of Leadership," in *The Leader-Manager*, ed. John N. Williamson (New York: John Wiley & Sons, 1984), 79–89.
2. Edwin H. Friedman, *Generation to Generation* (New York: Guilford Press, 1985), 79–89.
3. James MacGregor Burns, *Leadership* (New York: Harper & Row, 1978), 50.
4. Edwin P. Hollander and Jan Yoder, "Some Issues in Comparing Women and Men as Leaders," in *Contemporary Issues in Leadership*, ed. William E. Rosenbach and Robert L. Taylor (Boulder: Westview Press, 1984), 235.
5. John Naisbitt, *Megatrends* (New York: Warner Books, 1982), chaps. 2, 7, 8.
6. Marilyn Loden, *Feminine Leadership: Or How to Succeed in Business without Being One of the Boys* (New York: Times Books, 1985).

7. Marilyn Loden, "Feminine Leadership," *Vital Speeches* 52 (May 15, 1986):473.
8. Loden, *Feminine Leadership*, 26, 63.
9. Ibid., 4.
10. Alice Sargent, *The Androgynous Manager* (New York: AMACOM, 1981).
11. John Naisbitt and Patricia Aburdene, *Re-inventing the Corporation* (New York: Warner Books, 1985), 207.
12. *Applied Management Newsletter* 8 (January 1985):1.
13. Janet O. Hagberg, *Real Power* (Minneapolis: Winston Press, 1984), 149.
14. Ibid., 168–69.

CHAPTER 8: PASTORS ARE ALSO LEADERS

1. Lyle E. Schaller, *The Multiple Staff in the Larger Church* (Nashville: Abingdon Press, 1980), 106.
2. E. Mansell Pattison, *Pastor and Parish—A Systems Approach* (Philadelphia: Fortress Press, 1977), 48.
3. Richard D. Vangerud, "The Ministry Today: A Survey of Perspectives," *Word and World* 1 (Fall 1981): 391–97.
4. Ibid., 397.
5. Margaret Fletcher Clark and Loren Mead, "Ten Models of Ordained Ministry," *Action Information* 9 (November-December 1983):104.
6. H. Richard Niebuhr, *The Purpose of the Church and Its Ministry* (New York: Harper & Row, 1956), 51.
7. Ibid., 57.
8. Ibid., 79.
9. Lyle E. Schaller, *Getting Things Done* (Nashville: Abingdon Press, 1986), 99.
10. Kennon L. Callahan, *Twelve Keys to an Effective Church* (San Francisco: Harper & Row, 1983), 41.
11. Ibid., 41–42.
12. Edward H. Koster, "Leader Relationships: A Key to Congregational Size," *Action Information* 8 (January-February 1987):1–5.
13. Myrna Christopher Kysar, *The Pastor as Servant-Leader* (Minneapolis: Augsburg, 1987), 26.

CHAPTER 9: LAY LEADERS IN THE CHURCH

1. "The Installation of Elected Parish Officers," in *Occasional Services* (Minneapolis: Augsburg, 1982), 134.

2. Norman R. DePuy, "Responsibility and Authority in the Church," *The Christian Ministry* 18 (March 1987):8.

CHAPTER 10: THE LEADERSHIP TEAM

1. John Naisbitt, *Megatrends* (New York: Warner Books, 1982), 198.
2. John Naisbitt and Patricia Aburdene, *Re-inventing the Corporation* (New York: Warner Books, 1985), 62.
3. John W. Gardner, *The Nature of Leadership* (Washington D. C.: Independent Sector, 1986), 15.
4. "Getting It Together in the Team," a two-part article in *The Center Letter* 2, nos. 13 & 14 (Nov. & Dec. 1972), ed. Charles H. Ellzey and Paul M. Dietterich, Center for Parish Development, Chicago, Ill. The Center for Parish Development is a church research agency focusing on the processes of planned transformation. *The Center Letter* is a monthly research publication available on a subscription basis.
5. Herman J. Sweet, *The Multiple Staff in the Local Church* (Philadelphia: Westminster Press, 1963), 44.
6. *The Personnel Manual*, Lutheran Church of the Good Shepherd, Minneapolis.
7. Douglas McGregor, *The Professional Manager* (New York: McGraw-Hill, 1967), 169.
8. Charles Garfield, *Peak Performers* (New York: Avon Books, 1986), 182.
9. *Personnel Manual.*
10. Kenneth R. Mitchell, *Psychological and Theological Relationships in the Multiple Staff Ministry* (Philadelphia: Westminster Press, 1966), 173.
11. Ibid., 179.
12. James C. Fenhagen, *Mutual Ministry* (New York: Seabury Press, 1977), 103.
13. Adapted from *Applied Management Newsletter* 7 (August 1984).

CHAPTER 11: VISIONING AND PLANNING

1. Robert K. Greenleaf, *Servant Leadership* (New York: Paulist Press, 1977), 16.
2. Warren Bennis and Burt Nanus, *Leaders: The Strategies for Taking Charge* (New York: Harper & Row, 1985), 28.
3. Ibid., 90-91.
4. Charles Garfield, *Peak Performers* (New York: Avon Books, 1986), 110.

5. Tom Peters and Nancy Austin, *A Passion for Excellence* (New York: Random House, 1985), 284.
6. Daniel V. Biles III, "Pursuing Excellence in Ministry," *Lutheran Partners* 3 (July/August 1987):15.
7. Peters and Austin, *Passion for Excellence*, 286.
8. Bennis and Nanus, *Leaders*, 96.
9. Ibid., 103.
10. Jurgen Moltmann, *The Theology of Hope* (New York: Harper & Row, 1967), 16.
11. Jurgen Moltmann, *Hope and Planning* (New York: Harper & Row, 1971), 178, 194.
12. Ibid., 198.
13. Edward R. Dayton and Ted W. Engstrom, *Strategy For Leadership* (Old Tappan, N. J.: Fleming H. Revell Company, 1979), 78.
14. Ibid., 79.
15. Ibid.
16. Lyle E. Schaller, *Effective Church Planning* (Nashville: Abingdon Press, 1979), 101-3.
17. Ibid.
18. Lyle E. Schaller, "A Practitioner's Perspective," in *Building Effective Ministry*, ed. Carl S. Dudley (San Francisco: Harper & Row, 1983), 166.
19. John K. Clemens and Douglas F. Mayer, *The Classic Touch* (Homewood: Dow Jones-Irwin, 1987), 18.
20. Robert F. Mager, *Goal Analysis* (Belmont: Fearson Publishers, 1972), 29.
21. Dayton and Engstrom, *Strategy For Leadership*, 56-58.
22. Alvin J. Lindgren and Norman Shawchuck, *Let My People Go* (Nashville: Abingdon Press, 1981), 96-97.

CHAPTER 12: MOTIVATING

1. Thomas J. Peters and Robert H. Waterman, Jr., *In Search of Excellence* (New York: Harper & Row, 1982), 55-86.
2. Abraham H. Maslow, *Motivation and Personality* (Third ed.; New York: Harper & Row, 1970), 35-104.
3. Adapted from *Managing Interpersonal Relationships* (Minneapolis: Wilson Learning, 1980), 12-13.

4. Frederick Herzberg, *Work and the Nature of Man* (New York: World Publishing Company, 1966), 129.
5. David C. McClelland, *The Achievement Motive* (New York: Appleton-Century-Crofts, 1955).
6. Victor H. Vroom, *Work and Motivation* (New York: John Wiley & Sons, 1964).
7. Adapted from *Training Volunteer Leaders*, Research and Development Division, National Council YMCA, 34.
8. James MacGregor Burns, *Leadership* (New York: Harper & Row, 1978), 20.
9. Ibid., 19.
10. Ibid., 425–26.
11. Ibid., 452.
12. Ibid.
13. *Training Volunteer Leaders*, 125.

CHAPTER 13: MANAGING CONFLICT

1. G. W. Garvin, "Marks of Growing Churches," *Action Information* 11 (August-September 1985):1–4.
2. Quoted by Martin E. Marty in *Context* 18 (November 1, 1986):1–2.
3. Kenneth Haugk and William McKay, "Dealing With Parish Antagonists," *The Circuit Rider* 4 (July-August 1980):3–5.
4. Peg Meier, "Dealing With Difficult People," *Minneapolis Star Tribune*, March 24, 1987, 1C.
5. *Applied Management Newsletter* 10 (December 1986):1.
6. "Interview With Cecil Osborne," *Your Church* 33 (May-June 1987):16.
7. Ibid.
8. Ibid., 39.
9. "When Conflict Erupts in Your Church," interview with Speed Leas in *Action Information* 11 (September-October 1985):16–17; see also "Conflict in the Parish: How Bad is It?" *Word & World* 4 (Spring 1984):182–91.
10. Roger Fisher and William Ury, *Getting to Yes* (New York: Penguin Books, 1983), 21.
11. Ibid., 43.
12. Ibid., 83.
13. Ibid., 85.

CHAPTER 14: COORDINATING, ORGANIZING, AND STAFFING

1. Gibson Winter, *Religious Identity* (New York: Macmillan Co., 1968), 12.
2. Ibid., 105.
3. Peter F. Rudge, *Ministry and Management* (London: Tavistock Publications, 1968).
4. Ibid., 66.
5. Douglas McGregor, *The Professional Manager* (New York: McGraw-Hill, 1967), 162–69.

CHAPTER 15: LEADERSHIP AND SPIRITUALITY

1. Raymond E. Brown, *The Gospel According to St. John* (Garden City, N.Y.: Doubleday & Co., 1966), 1105.
2. Harlan Cleveland, "Essence of Leadership in One Minute's Reading," *Minneapolis Star Tribune*, June 30, 1987, p. 15A.
3. Edward C. Meyer, "Leadership: A Return to Basics," in *Contemporary Issues in Leadership*, ed. William E. Rosenbach and Robert L. Taylor (Boulder: Westview Press, 1984), 227–28.
4. John K. Clemens and Douglas F. Mayer, *The Classic Touch* (Homewood: Dow Jones-Irwin, 1987), xiv.
5. James MacGregor Burns, *Leadership* (New York: Harper & Row, 1978), 455.
6. Ibid., 462.
7. Warren Bennis and Burt Nanus, *Leaders: The Strategies for Taking Charge* (New York: Harper & Row, 1985), 93.
8. John Heider, "The Leader Who Knows How Things Happen," in *Contemporary Issues in Leadership*, ed. William E. Rosenbach and Robert L. Taylor (Boulder: Westview Press, 1984), 291.
9. Michael Maccoby, *The Leader* (New York: Simon & Schuster, 1981), 232.
10. Richard G. Hutcheson, Jr., *Wheel Within the Wheel* (Atlanta: John Knox Press, 1979), 243.
11. Ibid., 161–62.
12. Ibid., 161.
13. Ibid., 162.
14. Ray S. Anderson, *Minding God's Business* (Grand Rapids: W. B. Eerdmans, 1986), 66.
15. Ibid., 67.

CHAPTER 16: THE LEADER'S PERSONAL LIFE

1. Herbert W. Chilstrom, "The Pastoral Calling from a Perspective of a Bishop," *Word & World* 1 (Fall 1981): 335.
2. Herbert Butterfield, *Christianity and History* (London: Fontana Books, 1957), 189.
3. M. Basil Pennington, *Centering Prayer* (New York: Image Books, 1982), 202.
4. John H. Westerhoff III and John D. Eusden, *The Spiritual Life* (San Francisco: Seabury Press, 1982).
5. Howard Thurman, *Deep is the Hunger* (Richmond, Ind.: Friends United Press, 1956).
6. Lloyd John Ogilvie, *Let God Love You* (Waco, Tex.: Word Books, 1974), 72.
7. Ibid., 73.
8. David L. Fleming, *A Contemporary Reading of the Spiritual Exercises: A Companion to St. Ignatius' Text* (St. Louis: Institute of Jesuit Sources, 1980).
9. Fred Smith, *You and Your Network* (Waco, Tex.: Word Books, 1984).

AFTERWORD

1. Robert K. Greenleaf, *Servant Leadership* (New York: Paulist Press, 1977), 44–45.
2. Harlan Cleveland, "Learning the Art of Leadership," *Twin Cities*, August 1980, pp. 76–77.

FOR FURTHER STUDY

Adams, Arthur M. *Effective Leadership for Today's Church.* Philadelphia: Westminster Press, 1978. A very good book. General overview with practical application.

Anderson, James D., and Ezra E. Jones. *The Management of Ministry.* New York: Harper & Row, 1978. Focuses on the parish church and its particular community, guiding the development of ministry to the community.

Anderson, Ray S. *On Being Human.* Grand Rapids: Wm. B. Eerdmans, 1982. These essays in theological anthropology help one take a deep look at what it means to be human.

Bennis, Warren, and Burt Nanus. *Leaders: The Strategies for Taking Charge.* New York: Harper & Row, 1985. One of the very best. Full of useful insights. Clearly written.

Blanchard, Kenneth. *Leadership and the One Minute Manager.* New York: Morrow, 1985. A concise description of four leadership styles within the general category of situational leadership.

Blanchard, Kenneth, and Spencer Johnson. *The One Minute Manager.* New York: Morrow, 1982. Focuses on goal setting and motivation. Not deep, but practical.

Blanchard, Kenneth, and Robert Lorber. *Putting the One Minute Manager to Work.* New York: Morrow, 1984. A companion to the earlier book, taking its insights another step.

Burns, James MacGregor. *Leadership.* New York: Harper & Row, 1978. A 500-page study by the Pulitzer Prize-winning historian and political scientist. Distinguishes transactional from transforming leadership.

Callahan, Kennon L. *Twelve Keys to an Effective Church.* San Francisco: Harper & Row, 1983. Identifies 12 characteristics of effective churches and shows how they can be expressed in various settings.

215

Campbell, Thomas C., and Gary B. Reierson. *The Gift of Administration.* Philadelphia: Westminster Press, 1981. Emphasizes the idea that administration is one of God's gifts to the church and a means through which ministry is expressed. Good study of New Testament words.

Churchman, C. West. *The Systems Approach.* New York: Dell, 1968. Introduces and explains the "systems approach" to organizational life.

Clemens, John K., and Douglas F. Mayer. *The Classic Touch.* Homewood: Dow Jones-Irwin, 1987. Shows that leadership ideas are not all new. Many are expressed in the classic works of Western thought, including Homer, Plato, and Shakespeare. A different angle on the subject.

Dale, Robert D. *Pastoral Leadership.* Nashville: Abingdon Press, 1986. A handbook of resources that considers such leadership occasions as conflict, change, and team building.

Deville, Jard. *Pastor's Handbook on Interpersonal Relationships.* Grand Rapids: Baker Book House, 1986. Develops the idea that interpersonal relationships are the key to effective leadership in the church.

Doohan, Helen. *Leadership in Paul.* Wilmington: Michael Glazier, 1984. A scholarly study of Paul's leadership in the early church. Doohan says Paul combined Spirit-directed vision, strong personal conviction, and realism.

Drucker, Peter F. *Management.* New York: Harper & Row, 1973. An 800-page study by one of America's most influential writers and teachers on management and leadership. Good theory, and good practical ideas.

Engstrom, Ted W. *The Making of a Christian Leader.* Grand Rapids: Zondervan, 1976. A sweeping look at the leadership role. Begins with the biblical basis. Includes consideration of the role and activities of today's leader.

Ewing, David W. *The Human Side of Planning.* New York: Macmillan Co., 1969. One of the best on the planning process. Also details the process of implementation.

Fisher, Roger, and William Ury. *Getting to Yes.* New York: Penguin Books, 1983. A straightforward method of dealing with conflict without being nasty.

Fisher, Roger, and Scott Brown. *Getting Together.* Boston: Houghton Mifflin, 1988. Develops an approach to building good working relationships. Good book.

Fransen, Paul S. *Effective Church Councils*. Minneapolis: Augsburg, 1985. An excellent overview of important leadership principles and their practical application for a church's leadership team.

Friedman, Edwin H. *Generation to Generation*. New York: Guilford, 1985. Applies family system theory to church and synagogue. Excellent insights on self-differentiation.

Gardner, John W. A series of very good papers, 20–25 pages each, in the Leadershp Studies Program of Independent Sector, 1828 L Street N. W., Washington D.C. 20036.
   The Nature of Leadership (1986)
   The Tasks of Leadership (1986)
   The Heart of the Matter (1986)
   Leadership and Power (1986)
   The Moral Aspect of Leadership (1987)
   Attributes and Context (1987)
   Leadership Development (1987)
   Constituents and Followers (1987)
   The Task of Motivating Renewing (1988)
   The Changing Nature of Leadership (1988)
   Renewing (1988)

Garfield, Charles. *Peak Performers*. New York: Avon, 1986. Peak performers are average people who share six common attributes, says Garfield. An encouraging book.

Greenleaf, Robert K. *Servant Leadership*. New York: Paulist Press, 1977. This classic deserves to be on every church leader's desk. Emphasizes that leaders serve by leading and lead by serving.

Gustafson, James M. *Treasure in Earthen Vessels*. New York: Harper & Brothers, 1961. By focusing on the church as a human community, the author helps us see the necessity of leadership in the church.

Hagberg, Janet O. *Real Power*. Minneapolis: Winston Press, 1984. Hagberg's stages of power prompt self-understanding and awareness, provide goals for growth and development and provoke thinking about leadership.

Harbaugh, Gary L. *Pastor as Person*. Minneapolis: Augsburg, 1984. This book will help pastors know themselves—basic for effective leadership in the church.

Harris, John C. *Stress, Power and Ministry*. Washington D.C.: Alban Institute, 1977. This study centers on the relationship between

217

the pastor and the congregation, and shows how stress and power affect that relationship.

Henkelmann, Ervin F., and Stephan J. Carter. *How to Develop a Team Ministry and Make It Work.* St. Louis: Concordia Publishing House, 1985. The practical orientation of this book is based on sound principles and sound theology. Helpful appendices.

Heyd, Thomas. *Planning for Stewardship.* Minneapolis: Augsburg, 1980. While the focus is the development of a stewardship program, the booklet models an effective planning process.

Hickman, Craig R., and Michael S. Silva. *Creating Exellence.* New York: New American Library, 1984. Combines two big ideas in today's corporate world, strategic planning and corporate culture building. Excellent chapter on creating a vision.

Hutcheson, Richard G., Jr. *Wheel Within the Wheel.* Atlanta: John Knox Press, 1979. Good resource for understanding the leader's role in the various tasks of leadership, managing, coordinating, and negotiating.

Keating, Charles J. *The Leadership Book.* New York: Paulist Press, 1978. Examines theories and insights from managment and behavioral sciences and shows their application to church leadership. Basic and good.

Kellerman, Barbara, ed. *Leadership: Multidisciplinary Perspectives.* Englewood Cliffs, N.J.: Prentice-Hall, 1984. Twelve scholarly essays from the academic world. Various perspectives. Stimulating.

Leas, Speed B. *Leadership and Conflict.* Nashville: Abingdon Press, 1982. Building on theories of human need and leadership, Leas gives timely ideas for managing conflict.

Leavitt, Harold J. *Corporate Pathfinders.* Homewood: Dow Jones-Irwin, 1986. Discusses mission, purpose, and vision. Recommends a leadership mix that combines the vision of the pathfinder, the logic of the problem solver, and the action of the implementer.

Lee, Harris W. *Theology of Administration.* Minneapolis: Augsburg, 1981. Emphasizes that church administration is to be informed and shaped by theology. Relates secular tools to the ministry of the church.

Loder, Marilyn. *Feminine Leadership.* New York: Times Books, 1985. Focuses on the unique leadership strengths of women and the positive impact these strengths can have on an organization. A fine book.

Luecke, David E., and Samuel Southard. *Pastoral Administration*. Waco, Tex.: Word Books, 1986. The authors seek to integrate management and ministry. They show how administration contributes to the ministry of the church. Good book.

Maccoby, Michael. *The Leader*. New York: Simon & Schuster, 1981. Based on interviews with leaders who are working to make business and government more humane and effective. The result is stimulating and encouraging.

McConkey, Dale D. *Goal Setting*. Minneapolis: Augsburg, 1978. In just 27 pages this booklet covers the basics of planning in the church. States a rationale and gives step-by-step guidance.

McGinnis, Alan Loy. *Bringing Out the Best in People*. Minneapolis: Augsburg, 1985. Gives twelve guidelines for motivating people. Clearly written.

McGregor, Douglas. *The Human Side of Enterprise*. New York: McGraw-Hill, 1960. A classic. Develops Theory X and Theory Y scheme of leadership.

Moltmann, Jurgen. *Hope and Planning*. New York: Harper & Row, 1971. Moltmann's theology of hope is here applied to the planning process of the church. Provides solid theological rationale for church planning.

Myra, Harold, ed. *Leaders*. Waco, Tex.: Word Books, 1987. Interviews with 16 who excel in leadership. Encouraging and stimulating.

Niebuhr, H. Richard. *The Purpose of the Church and Its Ministry*. New York: Harper & Row, 1956. Viewing the church as both an institution and a community, Niebuhr paves the way for the use of leadership insights.

Nuechterlein, Anne Marie. *Improving Your Multiple Staff Ministry*. Minneapolis: Augsburg, 1989. Discusses expectations, staff covenants, self-esteem and the use of power. A good book.

Oswald, Roy M., and Otto Kroeger. *Personality Type and Religious Leadership*. Using the Myers-Briggs Type Indicator, the author explore the leadership implications of the various types. Insightful.

Peters, Thomas J., and Robert Waterman Jr. *In Search of Excellence*. New York: Harper & Row, 1982. Identifies the qualities of leaders in the top corporations in the U.S.

Peters, Thomas J., and Nancy Austin. *A Passion for Excellence: The Leadership Difference.* New York: Random House, 1985. Highlights the methods and accomplishments of those with special leadership ability. Both practical and inspirational.

Olsen, Frank H. *Church Staff Support.* Minneapolis: Augsburg, 1982. This concise booklet centers on cultivating and maintaining church staff relationships.

Roberts, Bruce B., and Howard I. Thorsheim. *Empowering Leadership.* Self-published, this study by professors at St. Olaf College centers on ways of empowering others for leadership. Much potential.

Rosenbach, Willima E., and Robert L. Taylor, eds. *Contemporary Issues in Leadership.* Boulder: Westview, 1984. Scholarly essays from various perspectives, stressing the dynamic view of leadership. A good book.

Rudge, Peter F. *Ministry and Management.* London: Tavistock Publications, 1968. To foster the theory and practice of church administration, this study reviews traditional positions and advocates the systems view. Becoming a classic.

Rueter, Alvin C. *Personnel Management in the Church.* Minneapolis: Augsburg, 1984. Basic insights for this important ministry. Includes appendices and examples.

Schaller, Lyle E. *Effective Church Planning.* Nashville: Abingdon Press, 1979. More theory than how-to; an excellent integration of Schaller's views. Describes various planning models.

_____. *Getting Things Done.* Nashville: Abingdon Press, 1986. For those who want to learn about church leadership in some depth, Schaller here addresses twelve practical issues. Wordy but helpful.

Somervill, Charles. *Leadership Strategies for Ministers.* Philadelphia: Westminster Press, 1987. Leadership principles and issues of interpersonal relationships are presented in story form. Reads like a novel.

Watermann, Robert H., Jr. *The Renewal Factor.* Toronto: Bantam, 1987. Centers on the vital role change has had in some of America's top corporations. A hopeful book.

INDEX